HUDSON TAYLOR
AND
CHINA

A DRAMATIC BIOGRAPHY

DAVID MALCOLM BENNETT

rhiza press

Hudson Taylor and China: A Dramatic Biography

Copyright © David Malcolm Bennett 2018
Published by Rhiza Press
www.rhizapress.com.au
PO Box 1519, Capalaba Qld 4157

ISBN: 978-1-925563-37-5

A cataloguing record for this title is available at the National Libary of Australia.

HUDSON TAYLOR
AND
CHINA

A DRAMATIC BIOGRAPHY

rhiza press

CONTENTS

NOTES

This is a genuine biography of James Hudson Taylor, though it has been dramatised to give the story more impact. This means that all the incidents recorded here happened, though some details have been imagined. In addition, while some of the conversations in this book are as recorded by the participants, most of them have been imagined, though they are based on the known thoughts and words of the characters.

Please note that when the word Mandarin is spelt with a capital 'M' it refers to the language. When mandarin is spelt with a lower case 'm' it refers to a Chinese magistrate or other official.

The China Inland Mission, founded by Hudson Taylor, served in several Asian lands. However, in this book it has been decided to concentrate primarily on its work in China.

Sometimes the China Inland Mission is referred to in these pages simply as the Mission, with a capital 'M'. However, when missions or mission in general are referred to a lower case 'm' is used. This is intended as a means of identification, not to elevate the CIM over other missions.

There are different systems of spelling for Chinese place names. The 'postal' system has been used in this book.

ABBREVIATIONS

AB: American Baptists
CES: Chinese Evangelisation Society
CIM: China Inland Mission
CMS: Church Missionary Society
LMS: London Missionary Society
OMF: Overseas Missionary Fellowship (the successor to CIM)

ACKNOWLEDGEMENTS

I wish to thank Sheron Ng, Ken Haron, Linda McKerrell and Mark Chapman of OMF International for their encouragement and help. As always I am grateful to my wife, Claire, for her comments on the manuscript, and for tolerating me spending so much time looking back to the nineteenth century.

I also wish to pay tribute to A. J. Broomhall for his remarkable *Hudson Taylor & China's Open Century* (7 vols. London: Hodder & OMF, 1981, 1982, 1984, 1985, 1988, 1989). It is a fine work of scholarship that I found extremely useful in researching the life of Hudson Taylor and mission in China.

David Malcolm Bennett (March 2017)

CHAPTER 1

HUDSON TAYLOR ARRIVES IN CHINA

A cannon ball screeched overhead and hit too close for comfort, smashing into a building with terrific force.

Then another did its terrible work.

And another!

Then gunshots!

They were followed by the screams of the injured, the dying, and those just terrified of what was taking place around them. China was at war with itself and at war with the Europeans, who were exercising an ever-increasing and unwelcome influence upon the nation and its people. That war had now reached Shanghai. It was not a good time or place to begin a missionary career. But James Hudson Taylor had landed in the middle of it.

It was March 1854 and parts of China were being devastated in the Taiping rebellion. Shanghai was in the hands of a group of rebel Triads known as the Small Sword Society. They had taken control of the city from the Manchus six months before and then, in order to stamp their authority on the city, had stabbed to death the city's senior magistrate. Despite this violence, the people of Shanghai had generally been sympathetic to the Triads and supported them: They were glad to see the Manchus go because their officials in the city had been corrupt and had taxed the people cruelly.

The Triad leaders often dressed in elaborate costumes to make themselves appear more regal and increase their authority amongst the people. This particular group wore red turbans and other brightly-coloured clothing and were often referred to as the Red Turban Triads. Most were also well armed. Some of the Small Sword leaders knew the Bible and quoted from it, but they appear to have been cultic rather than genuinely Christian. They were certainly most violent.

The walled city of Shanghai and its surrounding area had significant British, French and American settlements, which included various missions and trading companies. Amongst these missions were the London Missionary Society (LMS), the Church Missionary Society (CMS) and one run by the American Baptists (AB). The city was on the east coast and was a major trading centre. As such it inevitably attracted many undesirables from Europe, including fortune seekers and the more unruly of the sailors, and their behaviour caused friction between the Chinese and European communities.

The Manchus were now massing in the west and south of the city, with a force over 40,000 strong, and hoping to retake it. The Europeans and the Americans had declared their neutrality, but it is always hard to be neutral when one is in the middle of a war, living in or near a city under siege. The Manchus had attacked the British and American communities on the fringes of the city some months before Hudson Taylor had arrived, and, inevitably, the marines and sailors amongst the 'yang guizi' ('foreign devils') fought back. In fact, Hudson later said that the Imperial (Manchu) Army was 'a much greater source of discomfort and danger to the little European community' than the Red Turban Triads.

That was the world into which Hudson Taylor had arrived; a world of uncertainty, suspicion and violence. It was a dangerous place.

***

Hudson Taylor was a fresh-faced young man, of slight build, with wavy red hair and penetrating eyes. At this time, he looked little more than a boy, but he was a man of courage and dedication, proven by his being there at this time.

As he disembarked from the ship that had brought him to China, he felt a great sense of elation. He later wrote, 'My feelings on stepping ashore I cannot attempt to describe. My heart felt as though it had not room and must burst its bonds, while tears of gratitude fell from my eyes.'

The ship's captain directed him to the British Consulate, where he went to report his arrival and to ask for further directions. He had with him three letters of introduction. He entered the European-styled building and went to the front desk.

'Good morning! My name's Hudson Taylor. I have been sent by the Chinese Evangelisation Society to take the Gospel to the Chinese.'

'And what can I do for you?' The young man at reception was formal and polite, but not enthusiastic.

'I have just arrived from England. I wonder if you can give me directions.' Hudson handed over an addressed envelope. 'Where can I find Dr Tozer?'

The young man took the envelope and looked at it. 'He's dead. A few weeks ago!'

Hudson was shocked by that news, but he quickly recovered. 'And Mr Lewis Shuck?' Hudson handed over another envelope. 'He's a Bible translator, I understand.'

Once more the man at reception took and examined the envelope. 'He's gone back to America. A long time ago!'

Hudson's enthusiasm was beginning to wane. *Two down, one to go*, he thought. He handed over the third envelope. 'And Dr Walter Medhurst of the London Missionary Society? I hope he's still here and well.'

Once again the man perused the envelope. 'Oh yes! He's still here.'

Hudson felt his spirits lift. He knew that Medhurst was a leading figure in the mission community in Shanghai and a key man in the European community generally. 'And where will I find him?'

The receptionist gave Hudson directions. Then said, 'And be careful. This country's at war with itself.'

The new missionary thanked the young man and went off to find Walter Medhurst's home and surgery. He found it by late afternoon, but at first he could see no one at home. By this time Hudson was feeling lonely and downcast. Suddenly a young LMS missionary appeared and introduced himself. 'I'm Joseph Edkins. Are you James Taylor?'

'Yes, James Hudson Taylor.' They shook hands. 'I'm looking for Dr Medhurst.'

'Oh! Dr Medhurst is at the British Consulate today. I think I'm supposed to look after you.'

Hudson was not sure whether to be pleased or not. After all, he had just come from the Consulate. *Perhaps*, he thought, *that man at the desk didn't know Dr Medhurst was there.* However, Edkins seemed pleasant enough and appeared highly intelligent, though his uncertain manner was not particularly encouraging to a young man who had just arrived in a strange land. But it was a start.

'I think you ought to meet Dr Lockhart.' Edkins clearly did a lot of thinking. 'He runs a hospital to the north of the city. I'll take you to see him.'

'Yes, I've heard of Dr Lockhart. I'd love to meet him.'

'Leave your luggage here. We'll pick it up when we get back.'

The two young men marched to the hospital. Hudson was fascinated by the sights he saw. He gazed in wonder at the buildings with their intricate decorative work. He watched the people, hurrying hither and thither. The traffic was mainly horse-drawn, but there were men pushing wheelbarrows stacked with luggage and merchandise, while the rich travelled in sedan chairs. (Rickshaws did not appear until some years later.) Some of the narrower stone-lined streets had banners crossing their entire width, proclaiming messages unreadable to the new missionary. Everywhere there was haste and activity as people went about their business. Some stared at the two Englishmen, dressed in their strange western clothes. The sounds of war still confronted them, but they were in no immediate danger.

They arrived at the hospital and walked through the doorway. The sights, sounds and smells struck Hudson Taylor powerfully. The hospital served all: missionary staff, European officials, sick sailors, and ill or wounded Chinese. The war had greatly increased the number from that final group, so the hospital was crowded.

The two young men walked through the wards, until they saw a tall, strongly built man, examining a patient. Edkins walked towards him, followed by Taylor.

They waited until he had finished and then Edkins approached him, with Hudson in tow. 'Dr Lockhart, James Taylor has just arrived from England. I thought you ought to meet him.'

'Ah, Taylor! Yes! We heard you were coming.' William Lockhart spoke with authority. Both his size and his manner made him a man not to be ignored. He stretched out a powerful, but slender hand, which the new arrival shook. 'You have a little medical training I hear?'

'Yes, sir!' responded Hudson, a little less confident than usual.

'That will make you even more useful. I must press on. Lots of patients at the moment! The war, you know. Look, stay with me until you find other accommodation. I will be pleased to have you. My wife's back in England for a while.'

'Thank you, Dr Lockhart. That is kind.'

'Edkins will take you there. See you later then. God keep you safe!'

The two young men left the hospital and Edkins took Hudson Taylor to Lockhart's home nearby. 'I will see that your luggage is delivered this evening. Make sure everything arrives safely. Let me know if it doesn't. Sometimes things just disappear.'

Hudson smiled. 'And what do you do for the Lord? What area of service?'

'Well, I'm good with languages, so I've produced some Scripture tracts in Mandarin. There are different dialects, you know, so you have to be careful that you get it right. Not always easy! I evangelise too, using the tracts.'

'I see.'

It was dark now, but they kept walking and eventually arrived at Lockhart's home. Edkins opened the door and escorted Hudson to his room. Hudson noticed what seemed to be an excess of mattresses. He stared at them.

'Ah!' said Edkins, noticing his surprise. 'Those are in case a cannon ball hits us. You sleep on one mattress and surround yourself with the others. They hopefully will give you some protection if the worst happens.'

'Oh, I see.'

'And make sure you sleep with your clothes and valuables close at hand. If you have to make a quick escape, you don't want to spend time looking for them.'

Later that evening Hudson Taylor's luggage arrived safely. William Lockhart also returned to his home and they had their evening meal.

That night Hudson found sleep difficult. It was partly the excitement of at last having arrived in China, but it was more that the sounds of war were loud enough to wake the dead. A little later he wrote to his family, saying, 'They are fighting now, and the house shakes again with the noise of the reports.'

CHAPTER 2

HUDSON TAYLOR

'No conversion ever takes place save by the almighty power of the Holy Ghost' (Hudson Taylor).

Methodism had come into being in Britain through the evangelical revival of the eighteenth century. John and Charles Wesley and George Whitefield had been the leading figures in its origins and rising, though a doctrinal split between the Wesleys and Whitefield did divide it into two factions. At the death of John Wesley in 1791 there were over 72,000 Wesleyan Methodists in Great Britain and Ireland. In the next 40 years, British Methodism again divided, but exploded in a sequence of revivals that saw the different factions that emerged from Wesleyan Methodism grow to about 325,000 in total.

The Taylor family were Methodists and some of their ancestors had played significant parts in the rapid development of that movement. They lived in Barnsley, in the northern English county of Yorkshire. James Taylor Sr (1749-95) had played host to John Wesley and became a Methodist local preacher himself. His son, John Taylor (1778-1834), was a Methodist class-leader, and had married Mary Shepherd. Mary was the daughter or grand-daughter of William Shepherd, who had accompanied John Wesley on his travels in the summer and autumn of 1745.

John and Mary's son, James Taylor Jr (1807-81), married Amelia Hudson (1808-81), the daughter of a Methodist minister. James Taylor Jr was a pharmacist and a Methodist local preacher. The first child of James and Amelia was born on 21 May 1832. They called him James Hudson Taylor.

James and Amelia Taylor prayed for their son before he was born. They prayed that he would become a missionary to China. The boy was brought up, then, in a devout Methodist home. The father was an intelligent man and read a lot of books on such subjects as medicine and theology, plus many about missionary work. In fact, the adventures of overseas missionaries and the call of Christ were common topics of family conversation. Four other children were born to the family, two boys who died young, and two girls, Amelia, named after her mother, and Louisa. Hudson was always closer to Amelia, the eldest of the two sisters. From early on he seems to have been called Hudson in the family, presumably to distinguish him from his father.

The Taylor children were schooled at home, at least in their early years. Their father taught them arithmetic, Latin and French, and their mother, who was also highly intelligent, taught them English, music and natural history. Their educational methods were progressive. In an age of educational strictness and routine, Mr and Mrs Taylor allowed their children, under parental guidance, to play, read, explore and learn for themselves. Hudson did go to a formal school for two years from the age of eleven, but left to help his father in the pharmacy, which was an education in itself.

When Hudson was eleven the family acquired a book by Peter Parley, called *China and the Chinese*. The young Hudson Taylor read it so often that he memorised whole sections of it. In fact, memorising was a common aspect of life in the Taylor household. Hudson's father had a remarkable memory, which he put to effective use.

Parley, in his book, said that China was 'one of the most interesting nations on the face of the earth.' Hudson read that and as he continued reading he came to agree with Parley: China was, indeed, 'most interesting.' Parley also called China '*one of the* most wonderful countries in the world' and he even hinted that it might be '*the* most wonderful.' Hudson found it hard to disagree. Parley next highlighted many of the remarkable things the Chinese had achieved and discovered, and then, strikingly, he said, 'the Chinese, with all their great advantages, are not a *great* nation. They go on from age to age without making any progress.'

Why is that? Hudson asked the non-present Parley. Parley answered in the book. The failure to become a great nation was because of 'a false system of religion and government.' That sent the young boy's mind racing. Maybe he could do nothing about the government, but what about the religion. He began to realise that the Chinese people needed Christianity, but, more than that, they needed Jesus Christ. Those thoughts stayed with him for some time, then faded, only to rise again and dominate his thinking.

In his teens Hudson, in his own words, 'tried to make myself a Christian'. He failed, like everyone else who embarks upon that futile quest and subsequently began to conclude that he could not be saved. He also noted that it was common at that time for people to describe a conversion experience as 'becoming serious,' and he later said that far too many Christians seemed to be 'very serious,' unpleasantly so. (Strangely, another name given to conversion in Methodist circles at that time was 'made happy.') As a result of his failure to convert himself, along with his negative feelings toward all this seriousness, Hudson adopted sceptical views in his early teens and began mixing with like-minded young people.

At the age of fifteen Hudson went to work in a bank. His father thought bookkeeping skills would be useful to him and, presumably, the family business. The bank did not prove to be a good environment for a young man seeking the truth. There were plenty of sceptics there and they laughed at Hudson's half-hearted Christianity.

'Read the Bible today, Hudson? Preached any good sermons? You're nothing but an old Methody.' The taunts were never ending. Hudson blushed with embarrassment and found himself wishing that he was not a 'Methody', young or old.

But on it went. 'Why don't you come to the races with us. You'll win yourself a fortune.'

That did sound exciting. Hudson loved horses, and money was always attractive, but he knew his father would not approve. Nor his mother, or sister, Amelia! Yet he did not want to sound as though he was against people enjoying themselves. 'I might just do that,' he replied, with a defiant look, but he was not sure that he ever would.

It was probably just as well that his career at the bank soon ended, which it did in strange circumstances. He began to have trouble with his eyes while trying to do the accounts by candlelight. He later recalled, 'My eyes gave out at balancing time.' So, after just nine months he left banking never to return, and went back to his father's pharmacy.

One day a little later he found himself alone at home with nothing to do. His mother was away and his father was at work. He entered his father's library, looked at the books, saw nothing that particularly attracted him on the shelves, and instead picked out a tract from a basket on a table. Knowing how tracts functioned, he thought, *There'll be a story at the beginning and a sermon or moral at the end. I'll read the former and leave the latter for those who like it.* So, he read the story.

That afternoon, over 100 kilometres away, his mother found herself with more leisure than she would have had at home, so she decided to pray for the conversion of her son and to continue doing so until she believed that her prayer had been answered. She prayed and prayed and prayed for her son, then stopped.

Meanwhile, back home, Hudson was reading the tract. He read the story about a dying coalman and his wife, and was powerfully struck by the sentence: 'The finished work of Christ.' His mind began to race. Having been raised in a Christian family and knowing the Scriptures well, immediately our Lord's words on the cross flashed through his mind. *It is finished!* He next asked himself, *What was finished?* He thought for a moment and then concluded, *A full and perfect atonement and satisfaction for sin. The debt was paid by the Substitute. Christ died for our sins.* What striking thoughts! What remarkable ideas! Then in his mind he added, *And not for our sins only, but also for the sins of the whole world.*

Hudson Taylor was overwhelmed. He asked God, and he asked himself, *If the whole work was finished and the whole debt paid, what is there left for me to do?* As he later reflected, at that moment 'light was flashed into my soul by the Holy Spirit'. He fell to his knees, realising that he had to do nothing but believe in that Christ who had paid the debt, and trust Him for salvation. His mother's prayer was answered, and it was at about the same time that she was finishing her time of prayer in praise. James Hudson Taylor, a would-be sceptic, had been saved by Jesus Christ. What he could never do himself, Christ had done for him.

He began a fervent study of the Bible. He knew it well already, for, amidst all the books in the family library, it had always been *the* book. Yet now his study of it was on a new level, and he faithfully applied its lessons to his life. He also began to preach. He became an energetic evangelist and often counselled those concerned about their spiritual condition.

***

A young couple lived next door to the Taylors. Staying with them was the woman's brother, Benjamin Broomhall, who was three years older than Hudson. This young man was a frequent visitor to the Taylor home, and he found James Taylor's extensive knowledge and power of memory fascinating. Benjamin called Hudson's father the 'Oracle'.

Benjamin, too, was a Christian interested in China. Inevitably, Hudson and Benjamin became close friends. They shared their hopes; they shared their lives.

Broomhall also loved to look at the books in the Taylors' library. His sister and her husband had few books by comparison. But looking was not enough. He wanted to read them and asked if he might borrow some.

'By all means, young man!' replied Taylor. 'They're meant to be read, not just sit on the shelves. Take what you want, but let me know which ones you take; I might need them for my work.'

So, Benjamin Broomhall borrowed some books from James Taylor's library, especially his volumes on China.

CHAPTER 3

CHINA

'China was a land of mystery to most people' (A. J. Broomhall).

To most people in the west, China had long been a place of mystery. It had been a massive empire for centuries. In the thirteenth century, in the reign of Kublai Khan, the young Marco Polo had been the first European to penetrate its life with any success and return to tell the story. The tales he told on his return were so strange few believed him.

Chinese civilization had existed for 2,000 years before the birth of Christ. Over the centuries the various dynasties had come and gone, each making its artistic and social imprint on the nation's heritage. The Shang dynasty of the sixteenth-eleventh centuries BC was noted for its bronze vases and silk weaving. It was followed by the Zhou (or Chou) dynasty, which lasted around eight centuries, and for some of that time operated two separate, at times warring, empires, the Eastern and the Western. During that era bamboo books were developed, bronze work furthered and in 776 BC Chinese astronomers recorded an eclipse. It was also an era of social growth and agricultural development.

In 221 BC, Qin Shi Huang overthrew the Zhou dynasty, and for the first time united the whole of China. It was during the reign of the short-lived Qin dynasty, of which Shi Huang was the founder, that the Great Wall of China was built. Its purpose was to keep out the barbarians from the north. When Qui Shi Huang died, interred in his tomb with him were thousands of life-like, terra-cotta warriors, some with horses. These were re-discovered as recently as 1974.

Under the dynasties that followed, China did not always exist as one empire. Sometimes it was split into two, three or even more divisions. At times they peacefully coexisted, at others they fought fiercely.

The Chinese people were advanced and innovative. They invented the magnetic compass in the third century BC, produced paper around 100 AD, invented gunpowder in the tenth century and movable type for printing in the twelfth.

The nation's religion and philosophy appeared in varied forms. The first was Taoism, developed by Lao Tzu, in the sixth century BC. It was both a religious and a philosophical system. Its adherents worshipped different gods, and rejected excessive organisation and legal restraints. Taoism taught a belief in inaction, specifically that one should not react against aggressive behaviour, for such a reaction only furthered the aggression. It became the state religion during the Han dynasty, which ruled China for about four hundred years from about 200 BC.

Confucius was born in 551 BC, and his teachings were more philosophical than religious. In contrast with Taoism, he introduced various codes of conduct for the different strata of society, which emphasised justice, loyalty, propriety and respect for the Jun Tze (the Confucian ideal man). His aim was to promote a peaceful and orderly society. As the ages succeeded one another his teachings acquired religious trappings, influenced by the animist beliefs of many of his followers.

Around the middle of the first century AD Buddhism came to China. Buddhism was founded in India by Siddhartha Gautama, at about the same time that Confucius was developing his ideas in China. Gautama taught the four noble truths: that suffering is universal; that suffering is caused by desire; that desire should be eliminated; and that to do so requires the following of the eight-fold path, which included such practices as right views, right intentions, right speech, right conduct, right awareness and right concentration. Through a process of reincarnation, it was believed that the devotee would eventually reach Nirvana, which is virtual non-existence. The branch of Buddhism that entered China was the more liberal Mahayana form, which the Chinese further adapted.

By the early nineteenth century when Protestant Christianity arrived in China, the influence of both Taoism and Buddhism had declined, but Confucianism was still strong.

The first Christians to enter China were the Eastern Nestorians, who arrived not later than the 630s AD. They had translated parts of the Bible into Chinese by the ninth century, and experienced considerable persecution in the following period. Though their numbers declined significantly, there were still Nestorian services being held in China when Roman Catholic missionaries arrived in the thirteenth century.

Mainly through the zeal of Jesuit missionaries, the Catholics gained numerous converts from the sixteenth century. Imperial edicts periodically forbad Catholic teaching and at times persecution was fierce, but despite this it was estimated that there were about 300,000 Catholics in China by 1726.

The Manchus originated in the mid-seventeenth century in Peking (Beijing). They became the dominant power in China in the following century and remained so until well into the nineteenth. In the second quarter of the eighteenth century there was a rebellion against the Manchu emperor. He reacted violently against it. As some of those who opposed him were Chinese Catholics, he conducted anti-Catholic purges, which killed hundreds and destroyed many churches.

Then there were the Triads. Today the Triads are Chinese criminal groups, but originally the name referred to some secret societies, such as the Small Sword Society, which usually had revolutionary aims. Violence was a feature common to them. The number three and the triangle often featured in their thinking and ceremonies, hence the name Triads.

The first Protestant missionary to go to China was Robert Morrison, a Scot, who arrived in 1807. He had heard of the daring of William Carey in taking the gospel to India, and vowed that he would do the same for China. In 1804, at the age of 22, he approached the London Missionary Society (LMS) with his vision. He had a gift for languages and had already taught himself Hebrew, Greek and Latin, and had begun to learn Mandarin from manuscripts in the British Museum and from a Chinese acquaintance then living in London, who was trying to learn English.

The LMS eventually dispatched him to China on 31 January 1807 and he arrived in Canton, a port just north-west of Hong Kong, seven months later. His efforts saw very few converts but, working in secret for fear of the authorities, he translated the Scriptures and compiled a Chinese dictionary and grammar guide.

Very few brave souls followed his example. In fact, the Chinese authorities frowned upon and discouraged the presence of 'foreigners' in China, which made entry into the country very difficult. By the early 1830s there were only eight Protestant missionaries and missionary families in the whole of China, but by this time the handful of Chinese converts had begun to have greater success in presenting the gospel to their fellow nationals. But the population of China at that time was approaching 400 million, and the task ahead, with so little support from the Christianised nations, seemed impossible.

The great scandal of that time in British-Chinese relationships was the traffic of the drug opium. Opium had been used medicinally both in China and Europe for many years. In the mid-eighteenth century Robert Clive, who established the British Empire in India, recognised the commercial possibilities of that drug. It was being produced in the territory he governed, so he authorised the East India Company to commence exporting it to China.

It is probably true to say that the full social consequences of such traffic were not realised by anyone at the time. But as more and more Chinese began to use the drug the problems became very evident. In addition, with little other transportation available to get from place to place, some missionaries had used the ships that also transported opium. In the minds of many Chinese this put the missionaries in the same camp as those in this despised drug trade.

The Chinese had always been cautious about trading with the European powers, and they, quite naturally, were only willing to conduct such business when they believed it served their best interests. The drug trade obviously did not do that. The resulting disagreement between China and Britain grew to such intensity that war broke out. British warships sailed into Chinese waters and shelled Chinese ports. Hong Kong became occupied by the British early in 1841. On 28 August 1842, the Treaty of Nanking was signed, guaranteeing the opening of various major Chinese ports to foreign trade.

The war was strongly criticised by many in Britain. Dr Thomas Arnold, famous headmaster of Rugby School, described it as being 'so wicked as to be a national sin of the greatest possible magnitude.' The Christian humanitarian Lord Ashley (later Lord Shaftesbury) called it 'one of the most lawless, unnecessary, and unfair struggles in the record of history.'

But, whatever the wrongs of the Opium War, China was now open, not only to commercial trade, but also to missionary enterprise. Official persecution of the Christian Church had also ended, for the time being. From this time, Protestant missionaries began to enter China in significantly greater numbers. One of them was James Hudson Taylor, who had been sent to China by the Chinese Evangelisation Society on 19 September 1853. He was 21 years of age. That same day the British and Foreign Bible Society decided to print and distribute a million Chinese New Testaments. It was, perhaps, the most important day in the history of Christianity in China.

CHAPTER 4

THE PREPARATION

'The great need of every Christian worker is to know God' (Hudson Taylor).

At the age of 16 Hudson entered into a deeper, fuller experience of Christ. One day he went to his room and poured out his heart to God in praise and prayer, begging the Lord to give him some specific work, as 'an outlet for' his 'love and gratitude'. As he prayed, a 'deep solemnity' came over him, and 'the presence of God became unutterably real and blessed.' God was preparing him for a mighty venture of faith and China was again in focus.

Significantly, God had impacted other lives that were to have an influence upon Hudson's dream. Charles Gutzlaff, a German missionary to China, was one. He had become so fluent in Chinese and English that he proved most useful as a translator for British officials in that land. He became the Secretary for Chinese Affairs to the Governor of Hong Kong. He also founded the Chinese Christian Union, a ministry to the Chinese people, and was one of the first European missionaries to adopt Chinese clothing. In 1833, a year after Hudson Taylor was born, Gutzlaff had published a book called *A Journal of Three Voyages along the Coast of China in 1831, 1832 and 1833*. It is debated whether his own missionary work was successful or not, but there can be no doubt that he inspired many others to take the news of Jesus Christ to China.

In 1844 he founded the Christian Association for Propagating the

Gospel, also known as the Chinese Christian Union and Chinese Union. This mission to China encouraged Christians in various European countries to establish Christian work in that land. On a return visit to Europe, Gutzlaff met some British businessmen, who were so impressed by his story and vision that they began to publish a magazine called *The Gleaner in the Missionary Field*, which initially promoted missionary endeavour in various parts of the world. Later it focussed entirely upon China and it became *The Chinese Missionary Gleaner*.

Two of these businessmen were Richard Ball and George Pearse. Ball was from Somerset in the south-west of England, and he became the editor of the *Gleaner*, a position he held for some years. Pearse was a London stockbroker. He became a leader in the Chinese Evangelisation Society (CES), which emerged from the Chinese Union.

The *Gleaner* proved a most useful advocate of missionary endeavour. James Taylor subscribed to the *Gleaner* from the first issue. His son read it avidly.

It was on 2 December 1849 that Hudson Taylor decided that he should go to China as a missionary, but it was not all to happen in a moment. However, when *The Gleaner* began to appear it further nurtured that ambition. The first issue told him that there were only 50 Protestant missionaries in China and about 200 Chinese Protestant Christians, out of that population of nearly 400 million, and those Christians were almost entirely on the coastal fringe of the country. Thus, so far, only a tiny percentage of Chinese had responded to the call of Christ.

In other words, in that vast land there was less than one Protestant for every million of the population, so there were millions of people living and dying without even hearing about Jesus Christ. These thoughts filled Hudson Taylor's mind. They fired his determination to go to China as a missionary.

Hudson said that his parents 'neither discouraged nor encouraged' his 'desire to engage in missionary work.' They seem to have regarded it as a matter between him and God. Yet, aware of his convictions and ambitions, they advised him 'to use all the means in' his 'power to develop the resources of body, mind, heart and soul, and to wait prayerfully upon God' and follow His directing.

So, he waited. And prayed! But for Hudson Taylor, waiting did not mean doing nothing. He knew that part of the preparation for missionary work was doing the Lord's work where he was. If he could not serve God effectively in his homeland, he was going to be of no use on the mission field. Therefore, he engaged in teaching in Sunday schools, speaking about Christ in lodging houses, the distribution of tracts and visiting the sick.

Hudson also borrowed a copy of *China: Its State and Prospects*, written by medical missionary Walter Medhurst. That added to his desire to go to China. Medhurst's book also made him realise that acquiring skill and knowledge in medicine would make him more useful in China, and even more likely to be accepted by the people. He therefore moved to Hull, further to the east, and became an assistant to a doctor, Robert Hardey, who was associated with the Hull Medical School.

Being away from home and friends gave him more time to study the Bible. This he did with great enthusiasm. One of the lessons he learnt from the Scriptures at this time was the pointlessness of acquiring more and more possessions. He came to believe that in the way of Jesus Christ it was better to give than to own. This belief, he knew, would serve him well on the mission field, where he realised that he would likely move often, and an abundance of possessions would be a hindrance.

During this period, he also learnt to pray effectively. The kind doctor who employed him was, in Hudson's words, 'a truly Christian man,' but he seems to have been rather absent minded. Soon after Hudson had arrived in Hull, Robert Hardey said, 'Hudson, I confess sometimes I become so busy that I forget everyday things. If I ever forget to pay you, tell me and I will do so immediately.'

Hudson accepted this as a prayer challenge. He decided that if his employer forgot to pay him, he would not remind him. Instead he would pray and ask God to remind him. On one occasion, the time for payment came close, so Hudson prayed that God would remind the dear doctor about it. Hudson prayed and prayed. The time arrived when the money was due, but there was no payment. A few more days passed and still there was no payment. Hudson continued praying.

One Saturday he was left with one coin in his pocket, a half-crown. (A half-crown was one coin worth two shillings and sixpence.) On Sunday he went to church and during the day took part in gospel ministry. At the conclusion 'a poor man' came up to him.

'Mr Taylor,' he said hesitantly, 'my wife is ill. Would you come 'n pray for her?

'Yes, most certainly! Most certainly! Where do you live?'

The man told him and Hudson recognised the area as a downtrodden part of the town, little more than a slum.

So, the man led Hudson to that rough part of town, along a poor street and into a hovel, where he found a woman and five or six children, including a newborn infant. Hudson gazed at them and was in no doubt that they were all starving. His first thought was to give the man a shilling, so that they could buy some food. But Hudson did not have a shilling, only the half-crown, and Hudson realised that the man would not be able to give him change. He then thought about giving the man one shilling and sixpence, but the same problem blocked that idea. Hudson was wrestling with his conscience. He knew he should give the man the half crown, but was afraid to be without any money himself. Perhaps he should give the man two shillings! But again, that was not possible.

Hudson was stuck for words. He had made this visit to pray for the woman, but prayer alone in these circumstances seemed hypocritical. Yet, he thought, *I must pray*.

'You asked me to pray with your wife,' he said to the man, 'and I will gladly do so. Let us pray.'

Hudson knelt and began to pray. 'Our Father which art in heaven.' The words came out clearly enough, but he could not get the inner struggle out of his mind. *Am I mocking God?* he asked himself. *How can I call him Father when I am holding on to this half-crown?*

'Hallowed be thy name. Thy kingdom come. Thy will be done in earth as it is in heaven.' *But,* he thought, *am I doing God's will if I keep that half-crown?*

'Give us this day our daily bread.' Again he thought, *I can supply the daily bread for this family with the money in my pocket, but then I'd have nothing.*

'And forgive us our debts, as we forgive our debtors.' It seemed to be getting harder for him to utter each phrase, so confused was his mind, but he pressed on. 'And lead us not into temptation, but deliver us from evil. For thine is the kingdom the power and the glory for ever and ever, Amen.'

Never had he found it harder to pray. Never had he felt more guilty.

He rose to his feet and looked around the room again and looked the man in the eye. The man's face was full of agony and sorrow.

'Can you help us, sir?' the man pleaded.

Hudson Taylor reached into his pocket, pulled out the half-crown and gave it to him. 'Perhaps this will help.'

'Oh, thank you sir! Thank you.'

The sufferings of that family were, at least, temporarily relieved. Hudson Taylor later remembered that when he arrived home that night, 'My heart was as light as my pocket.'

The next morning, he was eating his breakfast, a bowl of porridge, which he feared might be his last meal for a while, when his landlady walked in carrying a small parcel. She gave it to him. He looked at it to see who had sent it, but the postmark and the return address had become smudged in the rain, so he could not tell. He opened it and found a pair of kid gloves. As he put them on, a coin fell out of one on to the floor. It was a half-sovereign, which was worth ten shillings, the equivalent of four half-crowns. His investment had been speedily returned with interest.

Another day passed, and another, and another and it was approaching the time when the rent on his room was due. Still he had not received his salary, but he kept praying.

That Saturday afternoon he was working with Dr Hardey, when the medic suddenly said, 'Taylor, isn't your salary due again?'

Hudson felt his spirits lift. 'Yes, doctor. In fact, it's been due for several weeks.'

'Several weeks? Oh! I'm so sorry. Why didn't you remind me? Oh dear, that's too bad of me. How much do I owe you?'

Hudson Taylor thought for a moment and made a calculation, which he relayed to his employer. But there was a problem. The doctor had just deposited money in the bank and had none in hand to give him. He explained this to Hudson and promised to pay him on Monday.

That evening Hudson stayed at the surgery and was preparing a talk for a meeting at a lodging house the next day. He was just about to return to his residence, when the door suddenly burst open. In rushed the doctor, his face beaming. 'Taylor, Taylor,' he said excitedly. 'One of my patients has just paid me. Here's the money I owe you.' He handed over some of the notes that he had just received. Hudson accepted them joyfully.

This was a crucial experience for Hudson Taylor. He was now strangely sure that he was on the right track. He was confident that the God who had answered prayer on this small matter, would answer it on a mission to China.

A little later he decided that he should move south to work in the London Hospital and his father offered to meet all the expenses, even though he was having financial difficulties. At about this time he met George Pearse of the Chinese Evangelisation Society. Pearse, on behalf of the CES, also offered to pay his expenses. In the end Hudson rejected both offers and moved to London, trusting God to supply his needs.

One evening he was sewing some papers together for a notebook, when he pricked a finger on his right hand. He thought nothing of it. The next day at the hospital he was involved in dissecting a severely diseased dead body. During the morning, he began to feel faint. He went outside and vomited. Then he developed a severe pain in his right hand. He reported this to his supervisor, who asked urgently, 'Have you cut yourself? Do you have a scratch?'

Hudson answered 'No!'

He then thought for a moment. Suddenly he remembered the night before. 'I did prick myself with a needle last night.'

A look of horror came over the supervisor's face. 'I am sorry young man, but you are a dead man. Go home and get your affairs in order.'

Hudson was shocked. At first he did not know what to do or say. Then he told the man, who was an agnostic, 'But I believe God has work for me to do in China. As a missionary, you know. I don't believe I will die yet.' The words came from an inner confidence in God and his purposes, but they were uttered hesitantly.

'That's all very well, young man, but my advice is go home and get your affairs in order before you are too far gone to do so.'

Hudson had insufficient money to hire a cab to go back to his lodgings, so he walked a good part of the way and when overcome with exhaustion boarded a bus. When he arrived home he lanced his finger to hopefully let out the poison and bathed it in hot water. He then fainted.

When he woke up he was in his bed. Hudson's landlady had advised his uncle, who lived nearby, about his illness. The uncle sent for his doctor and both men went to see the gravely sick young man. The doctor examined him, rather tentatively, then he and the uncle left the room.

'It doesn't look good, I'm afraid,' said the doctor. 'There is little I can do for him.'

'Is there nothing you can give him? Some medicine?'

The doctor thought for a moment and then rummaged in his bag and pulled out a bottle of coloured liquid. 'You could try this, I suppose. But I'm not optimistic. Keep him warm too.' The medic hesitated again and then added, 'And pray!'

The uncle did as the doctor advised. Hudson continued in a serious condition for some weeks, but gradually recovered. It was a remarkable answer to prayer. He later heard of the death of two men who had received similar wounds while dissecting bodies in another hospital at about the same time.

While in London, Hudson made frequent visits to Brook Street Chapel in Tottenham, then just outside the city, which was run by the Plymouth Brethren. They made him so welcome that he developed a great love for the Brethren, and many of them, in London and beyond, supported him in later years. Amongst the Brook Street Brethren was William Berger, a businessman, with whom Hudson was to have a close and important friendship.

As part of his medical training Hudson frequently had to care for patients who were dying. This was not easy, but he could never separate his medical responsibilities from his Christian concern. One of his male patients had gangrene and was not expected to live long. He was also an atheist, though he lived with a Christian family. Before Hudson had met him, a member of that family had sent a Scripture reader and the local vicar to see him. The man aggressively ordered the Scripture reader to leave and spat in the vicar's face.

But Hudson could approach the man from a different perspective. He was there to tend the man's gangrenous limb. Hudson said nothing of a Christian nature to him on the first few visits. He just cared for the man's physical need and tried to get to know him. At first it was not easy. The man had much to grumble about. However, after a few days it was clear that he had begun to warm to Hudson. After much prayer, 'one day with a trembling heart,' Hudson spoke to him about Christ.

'Let me tell you about Jesus Christ.' The words sounded rather confronting, even to Hudson. 'Did you know that He died for you? He died on the cross that you might be forgiven.' It was a start, but the man's face showed that he was not pleased.

Hudson saw the man's look but pressed on. 'Whatever you have done, whatever sins you have committed, He can forgive if you believe in Him. If you trust Him! He is the Lord and giver of life. He can save you.'

The man said nothing, but rolled over in his bed, with his back to the young evangelist.

Hudson realised that saying more at that time was pointless, so he made sure the man was comfortable and left. But he could not get him out of his mind, and he continued to pray for him. On each of the next few visits Hudson spoke a word about Christ to him. Each time the response was the same: the man said nothing and rolled over with his back to his helper.

One day Hudson visited him and tended his wound. Afterwards he had a struggle within himself. *Should I speak to this man about Christ again? Am I doing more harm than good by doing so? What shall I do?* He agonised over it, but he finally decided that this time he would say nothing. He made sure that everything was in order and walked to the door to leave. He glanced back, and there was the man still on his bed with an obvious look of surprise on his face. The look seemed to say, 'You have forgotten something.'

Hudson saw the man's expression and rushed back to the bedside, saying, 'My friend, whether you will hear it or not, I must deliver my soul. Let me pray for you.'

The man responded, 'If it will be a relief to you, do so.'

Hudson prayed fervently and then left.

Each time after that the man was willing to listen to Hudson speak about Christ. On one occasion the man said to him, 'I've not darkened the door of the church except once in the last 40 years. And that was when I was married.' He paused briefly, as if struggling with a grave problem. 'I didn't even go into the church for my wife's funeral.'

A few days later the man put his trust in Jesus Christ. From that time on his attitude was quite different. He was no longer aggressive. He was more welcoming. He was more thankful and his attitude to death had changed. He lived on for some months and died rejoicing in Christ.

Hudson Taylor was now an evangelist with medical training. He was ready to go to China as a missionary.

Charles Gutzlaff died in 1851. His vision and work lived on in James Hudson Taylor, but stretched further than even Gutzlaff could have imagined.

CHAPTER 5

THE TRIP TO CHINA

'God looked for someone weak enough to use, and found me'
(Hudson Taylor).

In 1853 the Chinese Evangelisation Society (CES) agreed to send
James Hudson Taylor to China as one of its missionaries. He was only
21 years of age. Early that September Hudson left London and travelled
north to Liverpool to board a ship for the trip that would change his
life, and, as it happens, change the lives of many others. His mother
and father also made their way to Liverpool to wish him well, as did
George Pearse. It was an important event for the CES.

Hudson was to sail in the *Dumfries*, a small, square-rigged sailing
vessel, with a crew of just over 20. Its main purpose was carrying cargo.
Hudson was to be the only passenger.

Yet all did not go smoothly. There were delays and yet more delays.
James Taylor had to return to Barnsley and Pearse to London before
the ship sailed, but Amelia Taylor determinedly remained in Liverpool.
The delays, however, gave Hudson time to search for and successfully
find some surgical equipment that had gone missing.

On Monday 19 September Hudson, his mother and a few others
assembled in a cabin at the stern of the *Dumfries* to pray for his welfare
and mission. They prayed and sang John Newton's hymn 'How sweet
the Name of Jesus sounds.' Amelia Hudson fussed. She inspected every
aspect of the small cabin to make certain that everything was in order.

She tested the bunk to make sure it was not too hard. She smoothed the bedclothes covering it.

The parting was fraught with sadness. There were no earthly guarantees. Ships often met disaster at sea, diseases commonly struck people moving to a new environment, and then there was the war in China. This might be the last time they would meet in this world.

'You *will* write, Hudson.'

'Yes, mother, of course I'll write.'

'You will write *often*.'

'Yes, mother, I will.'

'You won't take any unnecessary risks, will you?' That was uttered with a look of deep concern.

That was also more difficult to answer. What was an unnecessary risk? 'No, mother, I'll try not to.'

This is hard, he thought. *Even harder than I expected.*

'God bless you, my son.'

'God bless you, mother.'

The call came for the visitors to leave the ship. Amelia Taylor smoothed her son's bunk for the last time, held him in her arms and kissed him. Words would not come. Then, with a tear, she turned and left the vessel. Hudson kept his emotions under control, but within there was a mixture of excitement and sadness.

As the *Dumfries* began to leave the dock, Hudson climbed into the lower part of the rigging and waved farewell to his mother. She held a handkerchief in her hand, which she alternately used to wipe her eyes and wave to her son. As the ship pulled away he thought he heard her cry out, in what he called 'a cry of anguish.' Hudson felt a lump in his throat. Such partings were so difficult but so necessary in the life of a missionary.

***

The voyage began badly. A fierce gale hit them in the Irish Sea and lasted for many days. Conditions were appalling. Waves pounded the ship, which swayed and tossed in the giant seas. Waves smashed across the deck, soaking everything; visibility at times was almost zero. No one felt well. No one felt safe. Six days after leaving the harbour, with the storm showing no sign of abating, they became aware that they were in danger of crashing onto rocks. Their situation appeared desperate. For a short while even Hudson had begun to wonder whether his call to China was mistaken.

The ship's captain, a Christian man, was most concerned. As they drew ever closer to the rocks, he called out in desperation above the roar of the wind and sea 'We'll not survive another half hour.'

Then directing his attention briefly to Hudson, he shouted, 'What of your call to labour for the Lord in China? What of that now, eh?'

'Captain,' Hudson yelled, 'I fully expect to see China. The Lord will see us through.' These words were not bravado; they were uttered sincerely. Hudson had regained his confidence and trust that God was guiding him to a special mission.

Eventually the wind began to ease. The picture looked different, a little brighter. The wind still blew, the seas still crashed across the deck, but the fury in both had declined. Gradually through the night the storm abated, the sea stilled and they could move out to sea and towards their destination.

The rest of the long, long journey was accomplished without too many difficulties. They made what repairs were required while still at sea, and called in at various ports for much needed supplies. Twice they were becalmed for a while, but in these quieter times a breeze would spring up at night that helped them on their way.

There was, however, one more major danger that they did face. One Sunday they were not far from the north coast of New Guinea. Each Sunday the captain led a service. But on this occasion Hudson noticed that his mind was not fully on the job. Every now and then he moved to the side of the ship and peered over the rail.

When the service concluded, Hudson went up to him. 'Is something wrong?'

The captain paused for a moment, as if to work out how best to present the news. 'Well, yes, there is. This area is noted for reefs and we're in danger of drifting towards 'em.'

'Oh!' Hudson realised this meant danger, but was unsure how serious the problem was. In fact, it could, perhaps would, sink the ship with them still far from land.

'I'm going to let down the longboat. See if some strong rowing from the lads can pull us away from it.'

So, the longboat was let down. Most of the crew assembled in it, and they then began to row, trying to pull the ship away from the danger. But despite all the rowing the current seemed to pull them ever closer to the reef.

'It doesn't look good,' the captain whispered to Hudson. 'But there's no other way.'

There was silence for a minute or two, then Hudson said, 'There's one thing we haven't tried.'

'And what's that?' The captain wondered what a land-lubber could teach an experienced seaman.

'We could pray.'

The Captain stood stock still for a moment and said nothing. *Hudson*, the Captain thought, *maybe you are going too far this time.*

'There's you, me, the carpenter and the African steward. We're all Christians. Why don't we pray?'

The captain hesitated for a moment and then nodded. 'Alright, then. What do we have to lose?'

They rounded up the other two men and the quartet prayed. They did not pray long, for the situation demanded action as well as prayer.

When Hudson arrived back on deck the first officer was swearing violently and madly at everything and everybody. Hudson approached him with caution, but was daring enough to say, 'I believe a wind is coming. We should let down the mainsail to meet it.'

'Huh!' the seaman responded gruffly, looking at Hudson with contempt. 'I'd rather feel a wind than hear about it.'

It was then that a breeze began to blow, first gently, then more strongly. The captain by this time was also back on deck. He glared at the first officer. 'Let down the mainsail. Immediately, man! Let it down.' The officer did and the wind filled it. Soon they were being steered well away from the reef and the danger was over.

The rest of the voyage passed quietly. They arrived in Shanghai on 1 March 1854. The trip had taken more than five tedious months.

Hudson learnt an unexpected lesson on this journey. Before he departed his mother had given him a life-belt. Hudson was a bit embarrassed about it and gave it away. While that device would have been of no use to him in the storm in the Irish Sea and perhaps none if they had hit the reef, he still felt that he was not trusting in God if he kept it. However, later he came to realise that God uses means. He uses means such as life-belts to save people at sea. He uses means such as medicine to heal. He uses means such as walls to protect from flying debris. Sometimes God moves without observable means, but more often He works through the ordinary. A modern illustration would be 'Trust in God but lock your car door.'

So, James Hudson Taylor arrived in Shanghai, in China, in the middle of a war. It was a dangerous start to a remarkable career.

CHAPTER 6

HUDSON TAYLOR: YOUNG MISSIONARY

'All our difficulties are only platforms for the manifestations of God's grace, power and love' (Hudson Taylor).

Hudson stayed with Dr Lockhart on his first noisy night in Shanghai. Lockhart, recognising that the CES had no mission station in China, invited him to continue living in his home, which was just to the north of the walled city. Hudson based his activities there for about six months.

Hudson realised that one of his first tasks was to learn the language. He already knew a little, but nothing like enough to communicate effectively. He also realised that there were different Chinese dialects, so he needed advice on which one would be the most useful.

He approached Dr Walter Medhurst to enlist his help. Medhurst was a Scot, tough and durable. He was not just a medical man, but also an able linguist, who had written numerous articles in Chinese. He was also working with others on a Chinese translation of the Old Testament, to add to the New Testament which had already been published.

'Well, young man,' he said to Hudson, 'my advice would be to learn Mandarin. You could learn the Shanghai dialect, but that will only be of real use here. There are some similarities, but lots of differences. Mandarin, with some variations, is used through much of China.'

'Yes, that does sound best.'

'As you no doubt have already noticed we've a library here. Lots of useful books there! Make use of them.'

'Yes, I will.'

'But don't forget, the best way to learn is to listen to the Chinese who speak Mandarin. They're the best teachers, even when they are not trying to be. Mix with them. Listen to them. I'll also arrange for a Chinese teacher for you.'

Hudson hurried to the library, found some useful volumes, which included works by Medhurst, Edkins and Charles Gutzlaff, and returned to the Lockhart residence and began to study. Yet he knew that what Medhurst had said was true: learning a language was much more than studying books. He needed to get out amongst the Chinese and learn from them. He also soon made the decision to learn both Mandarin and the Shanghai dialect.

Hudson was introduced to a local Chinese Christian named Si who taught the missionary the local dialect. Up until now Hudson had met very few Chinese Christians and this close association with the middle-aged Si encouraged him as much as it helped him learn the language.

A little later, a Mandarin teacher arrived, and Hudson's language studies increased in intensity. They worked together for three hours each morning and three hours each afternoon. After a few days of this study he ventured out into the local shops to test his skills.

Hudson met with the teacher most days for several weeks. Then one day a Chinese servant rushed into Taylor's quarters in an agitated state. At first, Hudson did not understand the man's excited and garbled message, but he managed to get him to calm down and speak more slowly. What he then understood was that his Mandarin teacher had been kidnapped.

Hudson quickly looked for someone else to clarify the situation and found William Muirhead, another LMS missionary. 'Have you heard the news? My teacher has been kidnapped. By the Triads, I think.'

'Yes, I've heard. Perhaps a renegade band! Dr Medhurst is already after them. If we don't rescue the poor man they'll kill him. Or worse!'

Or worse! Hudson had a rough idea of what that meant.

Hudson and Muirhead rushed off in the direction that the bandits had gone. They finally found the group, each man heavily armed, with their terrified hostage kneeling before them. Medhurst was also there pleading for the man's life, but the Triad leader was unmoved. He claimed that they had found some papers on the man that linked him with the Manchus.

With difficulty Medhurst managed to gain a stay of execution and sent a messenger to report the matter to the British Consul. The Consul, Rutherford Alcock, quickly responded, sending a message that the man had been 'illegally captured on our ground' and should be immediately released.

The Triads began to argue amongst themselves. They were clearly divided about what to do. The Consul's messenger and Medhurst stood their ground and insisted that the poor man must be freed. In the end the Triads reluctantly seemed to decide that they had enough to do fighting the Manchus, it was better not to take on the British as well, so they let the teacher go.

Medhurst took the still terrified man home with him. The next morning, he had disappeared and they never saw him again. He must have decided that there were safer ways of earning a living.

***

From where he was staying Hudson could at times see the battle between the Manchus and the Triads. It was sad and terrifying, but exciting to watch. On one occasion, he was sitting on the veranda with another missionary when something suddenly whistled between them. When they looked behind them they found a musket ball embedded in the wall.

One morning, soon after his arrival, he decided that he would venture into the main city with LMS missionary Alexander Wylie, a linguist and printer working on Bible translation. Wylie was also an able evangelist.

Their nearest gate to the walled city was the north gate, which had been sealed. So they walked eastward and came across a ladder up against the city wall. The ladder was used for ferrying provisions into the city. Strangely no Manchu soldiers were anywhere to be seen in that area, so they climbed the ladder and entered the damaged city by this unorthodox route.

There were numerous Triad soldiers and others around, who were more than happy to listen to the two missionaries, so Wiley decided to preach. Nearby was a wrecked Buddhist temple, and Wylie used that as an illustration as he preached on the folly of trusting in idols. The people listened attentively, but sounds of a battle were then heard coming from the south of the city and the crowd dispersed.

On another trip Taylor and Wylie walked through the city streets and came across two Chinese men whom Wylie knew. They began a conversation, which Hudson listened to intently, though without too much understanding.

Suddenly a cannonball whizzed overhead and landed nearby with a great crash. The conversation ended in an instant and the four men took cover under the overhang of a building. Then they heard the whiz of another ball, followed by another crash. Then another!

The four men looked at each other and quickly decided that they were in the wrong place at the wrong time.

'I think we'd better make a dash for it, Hudson.'

'Yes, but where?'

'This way! Quickly! This way!'

They said a hasty goodbye to the two Chinese and departed towards the south. The Chinese men went north.

The two Englishmen darted from one covered spot to another, although none offered adequate protection. The cannonballs continued to scream in, but, as the missionaries moved out of the targeted area, gradually the sounds grew a little quieter and finally they ceased.

Later they made their way northwards to the LMS hospital. It was quieter now. The cannons had ceased firing. The few people on the streets were mainly clearing debris away.

As they approached the hospital they saw considerable activity outside its main door. There were numerous injured Chinese being attended to by the LMS staff. Others were being carried into the hospital. Some of the injured screamed in agony, while others lay there waiting for attention, or in silent acceptance of their fate.

When Hudson and Wylie arrived at the hospital, they saw the two Chinese men to whom they had spoken only an hour or so earlier. They were both in a bad way. Each of them had both lower legs severely damaged.

Hudson began helping the hospital staff and the patients were eventually all moved into the building. Dr Lockhart attended to the two men with damaged legs and decided that amputation was their only hope. Lockhart gently explained this to them through their screams of pain. Both shouted and screamed even louder in response. Their answer was clearly no.

Lockhart tried again, but before he had said a few words the two Chinese again became greatly agitated. They feared that this foreign doctor would kill them.

Hudson Taylor later recorded, 'Both died.'

***

But Hudson Taylor had come to tell the Chinese about Jesus Christ. While this terrible war did not make that easy, he was determined to do his job. In fact, it gave his mission more urgency. Here were people dying around him without Christ and he seemed helpless to do anything about it. What should be his next step?

When he felt that he had enough confidence to go it alone, he left the Lockhart residence and rented a house in a Chinese district and engaged in evangelism in the surrounding area. This meant primarily the distribution of tracts. He continued with this for several months. Throughout this time he had little money to spare and thus little food, but he was determined to press on with his work.

He had received little communication from the CES, other than some copies of the *Gleaner*, which he read avidly. While George Pearse did at times respond to Hudson's letters, he often failed to answer his questions. In the 1850s and early 1860s Pearse also served in other evangelistic organisations. He may have taken on too much to be effective in any of them.

The CES also sent him some financial aid, but it barely met his essential expenses. Hudson was beginning to feel cut adrift from those who had sent him. Fortunately, his family and Benjamin Broomhall wrote to him.

At one point in Hudson's first year in China, the French forces joined with the Manchus, which strengthened their arm. Cannons began to rain their shots down on the area close to where Taylor lived, especially at night. This made sleeping difficult, so Hudson decided to sleep during the day.

One night a nearby building was hit and caught fire. Hudson climbed to the roof of his house and looked in the direction of the fire to try to assess whether his home was in any danger. Suddenly there was the whizzing sound of another cannon ball approaching, followed by a bang and a clatter. It had hit the roof of the building next to his, showering him with broken tiles. Hudson took cover. The next morning, he found a small cannon ball in the courtyard, which he kept to remember his narrow escape. *God, indeed, must have work for me to do*, he thought, *if He protects me from even these dangers.* After that he moved to the European settlement.

All this was enough to frustrate anybody. He was in China to preach the Word of God, but here he was dodging missiles. Evangelism, for the most part, had to be neglected for a while.

Hudson later recorded in his *Retrospect*, 'The great enemy is always ready with his oft-repeated suggestion, "All these things are against me."' He added, 'But Oh, how false the word! The cold, and even the hunger, the watchings and sleeplessness of nights of danger, and the feeling at times of utter isolation and helplessness, were well and wisely chosen, and tenderly and lovingly meted out. What circumstances could have rendered the Word of God more sweet, the presence of God more real, the help of God more precious?'

Summer came and the heat was oppressive. Afternoon temperatures were frequently over 32° C (90° F), and sometimes much higher. He was not used to this heat and he became tired very quickly. There was also an outbreak of cholera in Shanghai at that time, and though Hudson escaped that disease he still had a bad attack of dysentery and kidney stones. Mercifully, the stones passed through, so an operation was unnecessary.

In fact, life was not easy for the missionary communities in southeast China. Nine missionaries in that region died within seven months of Hudson Taylor's arrival, including one woman who died six days after her wedding.

Apart from the danger of war and the problems with his health Hudson continued to be frustrated by his lack of fruitful ministry. In October, he recorded in his diary 'I have now been in China seven months and am almost useless as a missionary. I long for the time when I shall be able freely to speak of the love of Jesus.'

Yet there was encouragement. That same month he made a brief missionary trip with Si, the teacher, to nearby Wusong. On this visit, when Hudson's language failed, Si stepped in to help.

More encouragement came. Late in November Dr William Parker, another CES missionary, arrived with his family in Shanghai. Parker was a Presbyterian and 'a no-nonsense Scotsman'. With limited funds to rent a house, the Parker family moved in with Hudson. It was a tight squeeze, but there was no alternative.

European settlement and Chinese Protestant Christianity existed mainly in the coastal region of China. According to the Treaty of Nanking (1842), Europeans were permitted only in the ports of Canton, Amoy, Fuchow, Ningpo and Shanghai. In other words, Europeans were not allowed to go inland, but Hudson Taylor yearned to do so. Early in December he approached Joseph Edkins of the LMS to see what he thought.

'Joseph, I'm thinking of going inland, and taking the gospel to the people there.'

Edkins thought for a moment and then responded. 'Is your Chinese good enough, do you think?'

'Probably not! But no one is taking the gospel to those millions. Someone *must* do it, and I can go and give out tracts and speak as well as I'm able.'

Edkins thought again. 'Why don't we go together? My knowledge of the language is better than yours. I can preach; you can give out tracts and books.'

Hudson's face beamed. 'Yes! Yes! That would be wonderful. But when?'

'Well, not today, Hudson,' Edkins said smiling, reigning in the younger man. 'Let's plan for next week. We'll need supplies: Food, New Testaments and tracts! We'll have to get all that together.'

'Yes, that would be splendid. I'll start on that straight away.'

By the following week Hudson, with a little help from Edkins, had assembled the necessary supplies. On Saturday 16 December, they boarded a junk and travelled south along the Huangpu. After just a few hours they noticed that the noises of war had been left behind. In their place were the quieter sounds of junks skimming across the water and men shouting to each other.

When they came to the first village the people came out, but seemed rather nervous about this foreign invasion. After some smiles and a few friendly words, the villagers softened and greeted the two missionaries enthusiastically. Taylor and Edkins handed out some tracts, which some of the Chinese read carefully. Others accepted tracts, but looked at them in puzzlement. Presumably those men and women could not read.

As more villagers gathered around, Edkins decided to speak a brief word about Christ. The noise and activity quickly stilled and the people listened intently. When he had finished, one man invited them into his home and offered them tea, which was gladly accepted. Edkins agreed to keep in touch with that family.

It was then on to the next village and the next. They had similar responses in each. They then returned to their boat, and by morning the tide had taken them south to the city of Sungkiang.

They disembarked and began to explore the town. Inevitably, they attracted attention, and a host of people followed them. It was not long before they came across a Buddhist temple and they entered its courtyard. The crowd followed. It was too good an opportunity to miss, so Edkins preached and Taylor handed out tracts. The people crowded around Hudson, with hands outstretched eager to see what these two strange men were giving away. Even the monks listened to what the Europeans had to say and gladly took some tracts.

The situation changed when they left the temple. Out in the street they encountered a mob in an aggressive mood. The rabble moved in threateningly and jostled the two missionaries.

'Kill the foreign devils! Kill the foreign devils!' they screamed.

Hudson's Chinese was still limited but he was in no doubt about what was said, so he fully recognised the danger. Edkins had experienced it before and knew that a quick exit was required. They decided it was best to try to return to their junk. But deliberately or otherwise the mob blocked the way.

So, they made a dash for the river and ran down a side street, with the rabble in pursuit shouting and screaming.

'Quick! This way!' cried Edkins breathlessly.

Edkins led the way down another street with Hudson following and the aggressors chasing behind. Edkins had been to this city before and seemed to remember that this street led to a ferry pier, which would give them a good chance of escape. He was wrong. They ran through some gates and found themselves in a private wharf, with the river on one side, but no other obvious exit.

The horde of Chinese surged through the gates and stopped. They knew the area much better than the missionaries did, so they realised that their prey was cornered. They shut the gates and slowly began to move forward.

Edkins and Taylor looked at the mob and looked back at the river.

'The river's our only means of escape, I fear', said Edkins nervously. 'Move towards it slowly and pray that our God will deliver us.'

'Yes, you're right.'

So, the two men moved towards the river, keeping their eyes on the attackers. When they had neared the river a small boat passed by, close to the dock. Hudson made a sudden dash to the bank and leapt into the boat.

The attackers realised that their prey could escape, so they madly rushed forward.

As they did Hudson urged the shocked boatman to steer his vessel closer to where Edkins still stood. Mercifully the astonished man cooperated. When the boat was nearer to the dock, Edkins jumped in and the boatman quickly steered his vessel away to the other side of the river, where the two Britons disembarked.

The mob howled in anger, but they did not give up. They watched to see what the two foreigners would do next.

Taylor and Edkins had earlier agreed with the boatman who had brought them to Sungkiang to meet by a bridge further up the river. So, they began to walk towards the bridge. On the opposite side of the river the mob watched them. As the missionaries walked on one bank of the river, the rabble moved off in the same direction on the other.

The two missionaries arrived at the bridge, but their junk was nowhere to be seen. By this time the mob had arrived on the other side of the bridge. Edkins and Taylor were once more in great danger. On one side of the river the crowd was shouting and screaming threats. On the other side the two missionaries stood, not sure what to do. Only a bridge separated them.

Suddenly a Chinese man appeared. This was Dzien, one of the city's most respected scholars. He stood before the mob. It quietened immediately. He said something to the crowd that was barely audible to Edkins and Taylor, and slowly the mob dispersed. Dzien then led the two missionaries away to safety.

Later Hudson said to his companion, 'That was like Paul in Ephesus. There the town clerk quietened the mob to protect him. Here it was a local scholar. It's as well for us that the Chinese respect their scholars.'

Edkins nodded in agreement. 'Yes, it certainly is.'

After that they went south-west and visited more villages and after eight days returned to Shanghai. Probably at no time did they journey more than 50 kilometres from Shanghai. But it was far enough to give Hudson a taste of Chinese life away from a big city, and he had found it most exciting. This is what he had been called to do. This is what his mission should be.

CHAPTER 7

THE NEXT STEP

God's 'way of getting me out of difficulties has ever proved far better than any I could devise' (Hudson Taylor).

In 1855 it was still contrary to the Nanking Treaty for westerners to travel inland. However, some missionaries, including Hudson Taylor, decided to ignore that stipulation if the local Chinese authorities did not object. And many did not.

That year Hudson bravely conducted a series of short inland missions, initially about a week or a little longer in length, which were partly evangelistic and partly exploratory. The first began on January 25, where Hudson was accompanied by a couple of Chinese men, who were the crew of the houseboat he had hired. He took with him his medical bag and a supply of books and tracts to distribute as they went. They travelled east along the river and then south.

On the first afternoon and evening they made good progress and moored safely that night. When they awoke they found their little vessel surrounded by ice, but fortunately it was not too thick to break and continue their journey.

That morning Hudson instructed his companions to stop at the town of Chuansha, which they did. He prayed, grabbed a bag of books and tracts, disembarked and began to explore. It was a depressing experience as the war had devastated large sections of the town, but he came across numerous residents, who inevitably were fascinated by this strange foreigner. As they gathered around him he seized his opportunity and began to preach. The crowd grew larger and the people, for the most part, listened intently. They may not have understood all he said, but his skill in the Chinese language had greatly improved, so they still heard his message about Jesus Christ.

When he finished preaching he unpacked his bag of literature and began to hand out books and tracts. The people quickly gathered closer around him, jostled each other and eagerly grabbed the offered items. As each received a book or tract they quickly hurried off just in case this strange man wanted it back. As the crowd thinned he noted that some were slower to move than the others, and were clearly unwell. Several of these were accompanied by friends or relatives who were helping them.

Here was another opportunity. Hudson had not studied medicine for nothing. 'Come with me,' he said. 'I have medicine in my boat. I can help you.'

He began to walk slowly away encouraging them to go with him. At first none of them moved. They were, not surprisingly, suspicious of this foreigner.

'Come with me,' he repeated. 'I can help you.' He continued to move away slowly, gesturing to them to follow him as he went.

Then one or two did move after him and soon they were followed by others. By the time he arrived back where his boat was moored it was getting dark, and there were 12 people in a group behind him. He jumped on board the boat, quickly grabbed his medical bag and two small stools, and stepped back down on the bank. He sat on one stool and invited his first patient to sit on the other, and so, one by one, he examined all who needed it and treated them to the best of his ability. Most of the patients had malaria. After treatment each slowly moved off into the dark.

That night was colder than the one before and the next morning the ice around the boat was much thicker. This time they had to enlist help to break it, but as the sun rose the temperature increased enough to aid that process. They travelled south, remaining close to land.

The next town that Hudson visited was less welcoming than the first. As soon as he arrived in their midst the people surrounded him and behaved threateningly. Some grabbed him and examined his strange clothing. He later said, 'I was never more thoroughly mobbed.' He pushed his way through the crowd and began to walk quickly away from it. The mob followed. Hudson quickened his pace but so did the crowd.

Hudson had no doubt he was in real danger. 'Lord, help me,' he prayed.

God could help, would help, but he, Hudson Taylor, knew that he still needed to act, so he decided to return to his boat and get the crew to move off promptly. When he arrived at the place where the boat had been moored, it had vanished. He looked north and looked south, but could not see it.

The crowd had by now caught up with him, and stood a few metres away looking menacing. He saw some men standing by the bank, near where his boat had been, and in the best Chinese he could muster said, 'Where has my boat gone?'

These men excitedly babbled something he did not understand, but pointed energetically in a northerly direction. Hudson began to walk north. The crowd watched. He had not gone far when he heard laughing behind him. It was the men who had directed him. Hudson quickly realised that the laughs were on him, so he turned around and went south and soon found his boat with its crew. Fortunately, by this time the mob had lost interest and dispersed.

Hudson then went further south, visiting various towns, and reached as far as Zhapu, by the mouth of Hangchow Bay, more than 100 kilometres south of Shanghai. He had never intended this tour to be a long one, so he went no further. He and his crew restocked the boat and returned to Shanghai, arriving on the first day of February.

When he arrived at his home William Parker came out to greet him.

'Hudson! God be praised! I'm so glad to see you. You've been away longer than we expected. We've been worried.'

Hudson smiled. 'I'm fine. I've certainly had some adventures though.'

'Thank God you're safe. The Chinese authorities are getting more and more suspicious of foreigners. They suspect us all of being in favour of the rebellion.'

'Yes, I know. But I haven't come all this way to sit behind closed doors. I must get out there to tell these people about Christ.'

'Aye, that's true. That's what we're here for. Our meal is nearly ready. Come and join us.' The two men entered the house.

However, the prospect of danger from the authorities or the rebels did not deter Hudson Taylor. Indeed, living in Shanghai, a war zone, was no safer and food was in short supply, so he began preparing his next venture.

The next day he approached William Parker. 'Dr Parker, I'm thinking of going on a short mission to Wusong. It's just a few miles to the north. Will you come with me? It'll only take a day.'

Parker thought for a moment. 'Aye, of course. When?'

'Well, tomorrow!'

Parker's stern face broke into a half smile. 'Aye, I thought you'd say that.'

The next day they went by boat to Wusong. When they arrived they were greeted with suspicion, but once they began to offer books and tracts the people crowded around and took them gladly. It was a day well spent. They boarded the boat once more and headed south to Shanghai. As they approached the city they saw a war junk moving towards them, its sails flapping in the wind. Suddenly one of the sailors on board the junk raised his gun, took aim and fired at the two missionaries. The ball whistled past them.

The two men looked at each other and then back at the junk. The sailor had now lowered his gun and the junk sailed past without further action.

'That was a close call,' said Parker.

'Yes,' said Hudson. 'God must indeed be looking after us.'

'Aye!'

They returned home and Hudson considered what should be his next step. He first approached Alex Wylie of the LMS, one of the most experienced missionaries in the settlement. Hudson had greatly appreciated Wylie's help and advice when he had first arrived in China.

'Mr Wylie, I was thinking of going on another missionary journey. Do you have any advice? Any towns I should visit? Indeed, any advice on getting out of this city. It seems to be getting harder by the minute.' (The French in support of the Manchus had tightened their grip on the city.)

Wylie smiled. 'Yes, it is, isn't it? John Burdon and I are thinking of going to Tsingpu. Need permits from the Consul, though.'

'Right!'

'Why don't you come with us, Hudson?'

'Yes, I'd love to. So, when?'

Wylie paused for a moment. 'We'll apply for the permits today and hopefully be able to leave on the 16th or 17th.'

'That's good. I'll join you, God willing.'

So, they started preparing.

John Burdon was a CMS missionary, aged 26, who had arrived in Shanghai with his wife, Harriet, a year before Hudson. Sadly, Harriet had died in September 1854, leaving John with an infant child to care for.

In 1848 Drs Medhurst, Muirhead and Lockhart had visited Tsingpu and had been viciously attacked by a mob, badly beaten and held for ransom. The City Prefect had eventually sent a band of militiamen to rescue them. However, Taylor, Wylie and Burdon were each prepared to take whatever risks were involved in this trip.

They left Shanghai as planned on 16 February and went inland, journeying south west, in a small houseboat. When they arrived in Tsingpu 'a very rude mob' greeted them, crying, 'Death to the foreign devils! Death to the foreign devils!' Clearly the attitude of the people of Tsingpu toward foreigners had not changed in seven years.

The three missionaries looked at each other, wondering what to do next.

The mob kept shouting and screaming, and the more it shouted the larger it seemed to grow and the more threatening it became.

'Things don't seem to have changed much, do they?' said Wylie.

'No! It seems not', replied Hudson.

'I think we had better make a quick exit.' It was Wylie again.

'Yes!' said Hudson and Burdon in unison.

And quickly, but not too quickly, they escaped from the city the way they had entered it, found their vessel and pulled away. When they were out of immediate danger they stopped for a while, shared a meal and considered their next step.

'Let's move on to Sungkiang, as we originally planned,' said Wylie.

'Yes, we must,' said Hudson Taylor.

'Perhaps we'll get a better welcome there,' suggested Burdon.

The other two men laughed.

'Well, it couldn't be much worse.' It was Hudson.

So, they began to head further south and kept going into the early part of the night, before resting. The next morning, they continued their journey. Upon arrival at Sungkiang they climbed a hill, with views of the town, and sat in a derelict Pagoda to pray for the people, to sing praises to God and to read the Scriptures. When they had concluded they stepped out of the Pagoda and admired the view of the city and the surrounding area.

'What's that smoke?' asked Burdon, pointing to the north-east.

There was a pause as they scanned the horizon.

'It's Shanghai!' replied Wylie. He sounded a little puzzled.

Hudson smiled. 'There's always smoke in Shanghai. There is a war on.'

'Yes, I know, but not usually that much,' responded Wylie.

Sure enough the smoke was dense and widespread, and was clearly coming from the Shanghai area.

'I wonder what's happened!' said Hudson.

Wylie sighed. 'I didn't think things could get any worse there. But it looks like they have.'

There was nothing they could do for Shanghai or its people at that time, so they descended the hill and began to preach and distribute literature where they were. The people in Sungkiang responded very differently from those in Tsingpu. Many gathered around, listened to the missionaries and eagerly accepted tracts.

The missionaries continued their evangelistic efforts in Sungkiang and the surrounding area and returned to Shanghai a few days later. What they saw shocked them. Much of the city, which had already been devastated by war, had now been burnt to the ground. Fires still burnt in some parts of the city. Instead of rebel soldiers, Shanghai was now dominated by Manchu troops. Heads and savagely damaged bodies littered the streets.

They made their way to the mission settlement and William Parker greeted them grimly. 'It's been brutal. Terrible! The rebels set fire to the city and tried to make their escape. Some seem to have made it. But many others have been shot or hacked to death by the Manchus.'

The three men could not help but wonder what would happen next.

A mood of despondency came over Hudson Taylor as he reflected upon the new situation. There was such terrible suffering going on all around him and many dying without Christ and without hope.

He wondered, *What could I do, what could we do, in the midst of such conflict? Would the situation get better or would it get worse? Any improvement can only come from the hand of God.*

On March 1, James Hudson Taylor celebrated the first anniversary of his arrival in China. Yet 'celebration' was too positive a word, for at this stage there was not too much to celebrate. But he was hopeful. He had made giant steps in learning two Chinese dialects, and his conversation and preaching skills were improving all the time. His understanding of the Chinese people was also improving, and his grasp of the massive problem facing him and other missionaries was also now much clearer. But how could such tremendous needs be met?

CHAPTER 8

SLIGHT OBSTACLES

'We must not be hindered by slight obstacles' (Hudson Taylor).

In the next few days the newly triumphant Manchus put out the fires and began to rebuild the city. They approached the task with considerable vigour and skill and the city quickly arose from the ashes. It soon seemed as if the rebel occupation had never happened.

The Manchus also put land up for sale to raise money for the rebuilding. Hudson Taylor and William Parker, his CES associate, seized the moment and purchased a block of land, upon which they intended to build a CES headquarters and a hospital, even though funds were still in short supply.

Nearly a month after Hudson's travels with Wylie and Burdon, he launched out again, this time with William Parker. They first went north to Kiating, then south back to Tsingpu, despite the danger, and Changzhong, which was near Sungkiang. This trip had the twin aims of preaching the gospel and finding a suitable location for another mission site. It was not Taylor's intention to open a second site immediately, but he did need to work out where one could be established for future use.

At Kiating the people were curious, but nervous, about these two strange foreigners. They first observed them only from a distance. Then when Taylor and Parker began to offer tracts, the locals rushed them from all sides. When things had quietened down a little, Hudson preached briefly and offered to attend to any sick people in the town the following day. The two men then returned to their boat.

Early the next morning a crowd had assembled on the bank. Taylor and Parker looked out at the people before them.

'So many!' said Parker.

'Yes! And so many opportunities!'

Parker's face broke into a rare smile. 'And before breakfast!'

Hudson laughed. 'Yes! Not much chance of that for a while. I'll go down to them and see what the problems are. I'll deal with the more moderate cases and send the serious ones to you on the boat.'

'Aye, that makes sense.'

So, Hudson took hold of his medical bag and disembarked. The people quickly surrounded him. He began to question the nearest to find out their condition. He sent a few, one by one, to Parker on the boat, and began to attend to the others. As opportunity arose, he also asked them about whether they knew about Jesus Christ. It appears that a Roman Catholic priest did visit the town occasionally, so many of them were at least aware of Christ.

When they had finished their medical work they prepared a meal and ate. Afterwards they prayed for a while about their impending visit to Tsingpu. It was clear that missionaries, indeed any foreigners, were likely to be in danger in that town, so they were more aware even than usual of their dependence upon God. They then began to sort out some of their equipment and supplies.

'Have you seen my surgical instruments?' It was Hudson.

'Surgical instruments? They were in the cabin an hour or so ago. I saw them.'

'Well, I can't find them now.'

The two men searched the cabin and searched the rest of the boat, but could not find them or the case in which they were kept. They had vanished. 'They must have been stolen. One of the patients, I suppose.'

There was nothing they could do about the loss at that time, so they left Kiating and sailed on to Tsingpu, a little nervous of what might await them. On this occasion they disembarked at a different part of the town, and mercifully there was no 'welcoming committee' out to harm them. Instead they were warmly received. Offers of New Testaments and tracts were quickly accepted.

They made their way to a nearby temple, entered and were greeted by the priests. Some of the crowd followed them. Taylor and Parker offered New Testaments to the priests, which they accepted without hesitation. Hudson began to speak.

'I bring you good news,' he said. 'Good news about the God who created the heavens and the earth. This God loves you. He cares about you. This God sent His Son Jesus Christ into this world to show us what He is like. And to die for you.'

Both priests and people listened intently, though a few murmured comments to each other about this strange man and his strange God.

'He is not like these idols,' Hudson continued. 'They are just made of wood and stone. They cannot hear you. They cannot help you. When you are sick they can't heal you. When there is a famine they cannot bring rain, so that your food will grow. This book', Hudson held a New Testament above his head, 'tells us about the real God, the God who helps, who acts, who answers prayer. These idols can do nothing.'

Suddenly a man emerged from the crowd, and picked up a large stick. For a moment Hudson thought the man meant to strike him. But no, instead he began to dance around the idols and beat them with the stick. Others in the crowd laughed at his antics.

Hudson brought his brief sermon to an end, and he and Parker gave out some tracts and went back to their boat. God had kept them safe in this second visit to Tsingpu, and they had been able to present the gospel to its people. Their hearts were full of gratitude to God.

It was then on to Changzhong. There they were greeted by such a great crowd that they had to retreat to their boat to escape the crush. The people were not aggressive, but were so eager to get tracts and books that the two missionaries were knocked about in the melee. Despite the retreat of the two strange foreigners, the people still jostled with each other on the river bank to try to get the best view of them.

'Perhaps we should invite them on board,' said Hudson. 'In small numbers, I mean. Then we can speak to them face to face and give them tracts.'

'Aye,' said Parker hesitantly. 'So long as we don't let too many on at once. The boat might sink.'

Hudson nodded in agreement. He then signalled to some of the people closer to the boat, inviting them on board. At first nobody moved. Then suddenly one man climbed aboard and was quickly followed by more. As each person received a tract, they immediately departed and others took their place. When no one else dare come aboard, Taylor and Parker drew as close to the bank as they could and handed out more leaflets to people by the river.

They returned to Shanghai a couple of days later. The whole trip had taken only a week. However, these trips, brief though they had been, were helping Hudson Taylor form his missionary strategy. Now, more than ever, he realised that offering medical help was a great assistance to gain the confidence and interest of the Chinese people, as others had previously shown. This made him more determined to establish a hospital, but money and equipment would be needed.

Rev. John Hobson, the CMS chaplain to the British community in Shanghai, was the first to make a major gift towards that. He guaranteed Hudson Taylor £50 towards the proposed hospital. Hudson accepted the offer gratefully and praised God for it, but much more was needed. He had already advised George Pearse in London about the planned hospital, but had received no concrete response, so he wrote to him again. 'I hope you have taken up our proposal for a hospital with the vigour its importance demands,' Hudson told him. He also mentioned Hobson's gift, and suggested that this indicated 'the importance of the object to those on the spot.' He also urged Pearse to send more workers, saying, 'The door is opened wide; there is a great harvest, but few are ready to reap.'

But Pearse was busy. In fact, Pearse was always busy, too busy, and no response came.

Another area of ministry that Hudson engaged in was teaching in the tiny mission school, which catered for about 20 Chinese children. Mr Si, who had taught Hudson the local dialect, also taught in this school.

At about this time Hudson befriended a Chinese widow and her adult son Guihua. Like so many in Shanghai at that time, the war had left them penniless, but they responded to Hudson's kindness, and Guihua was keen to learn about Christ.

Hudson met regularly with Guihua, Mr Si, and another Chinese man named Tsien, helping them to understand the Christian faith. As time passed this group grew, as other Chinese became interested. When Hudson was travelling Mr Si led these meetings. Si and another Chinese Christian named Deng also helped Hudson Taylor preaching in the open air in Shanghai. The involvement of two visibly Chinese men may have made this more acceptable to the crowds who came to listen.

On the morning of 17 April 1855, Hudson Taylor began his most adventurous missionary journey yet. It was brave and dangerous. He wrote to George Pearse, telling him, 'we must not be hindered by slight obstacles,' but some of the obstacles he was to encounter on this trip were far from 'slight.'

His companion on this occasion was John Burdon of the CMS. This was a visit to the islands of Chongming and Haimen, situated in the mouth of the Yangtze, and the city of Tongzhou on the northern bank. For this they hired two sea-going junks, for they knew that sailing in sea conditions could be very hazardous. They also took two Chinese teachers and a servant with them.

They first went to Wusong again, a little north of Shanghai, though it was not their intention to stay there for long. However, their brief time there was long enough to confirm the ravages that the opium trade had made in China. They saw numerous shops selling opium, and evidence of people being destroyed by the drug was all around them.

It was then on to Chongming Island. By the time they arrived there it was night, so they bedded down in the junk and the next morning they moved on to the island's major city. Immediately they attracted a curious, even friendly crowd.

As the two men moved through the crowd to find a good position from which to preach, they came across an ancient shrine dedicated to Guandi, a war hero of the Han dynasty, who the people now regarded as a God. Hudson decided to use a tactic that the Apostle Paul had used in Athens centuries before. He moved to a higher part of the ground, where he could be easily seen, and addressed the crowd.

'I notice your reverence for Guandi, who served you heroically, so many years ago,' he began. 'But I want to tell you about another hero who lived at the same time in a distant place.'

The crowd had hushed. All eyes were on this strange foreigner.

'His name is Jesus,' Hudson continued. 'He is the Son of the one true God, the only God. He came to this earth to show us what this God is like. He healed the sick. He raised the dead. And He laid down His life for the good of the whole world. He died that we might not fear death, for He can give us eternal life.'

Hudson continued for a half-hour or more telling the people about Christ. When he had finished he and Burdon began to give out Testaments and tracts. For the first time the crowd became a little unruly, as people pushed and elbowed each other out of the way to get to the precious items. When the missionaries had given away all they had, Hudson cried out, 'We have more tracts in our boat. Follow us to the river and we will give you the words of life.'

So off to their boat they went, with dozens of people following them. When they arrived at their vessel they jumped aboard, found their supply of literature and began to offer items to those who had followed them. Once more eager hands reached out to grab the tracts, and the two missionaries had to move quickly to keep up with the demand. Gradually, the crowd dispersed and as the people wandered away each appeared to be examining the treasure that they had received.

A few days later they went to Haimen, a smaller island. But there some 'uncommonly rude men' surrounded them and though they were able to preach, they decided to move on. The next day Taylor and Burdon told the two Chinese teachers that they intended to go to Tongzhou on the main land. The two men protested vigorously.

'Tongzhou is a most dangerous place,' said one. 'The soldiers there are out of control.'

'You will both be killed,' said the other.

Hudson paused for a moment and ran his fingers through his new-grown, ginger beard. 'If it's that bad, we must go.'

'Yes,' said Burdon bravely. 'We've not come this far to retreat now.'

The next morning they sailed to the northern side of the river, disembarked and the two missionaries began to prepare for the journey to Tongzhou. They decided to leave the junks in the charge of the two Chinese teachers and take their servant with them.

'If we are not back in two days,' Hudson said to the two teachers, 'try to find out what has happened to us and return to Shanghai with the news.'

The two Chinese men bowed a little in agreement.

'Oh, and leave one junk behind, in case we return later.'

The two Chinese bowed again.

They moved off, each with a load of tracts and books. The roads they travelled were in a poor state. Walking in such conditions with the loads they were carrying proved very difficult, so they hired wheelbarrows and coolies to push them. After they had been travelling for some hours, their servant, who was clearly scared, asked for permission to return to Shanghai. They consented and he quickly disappeared. The wheelbarrow men continued with them.

A little later they met 'a respectable man' who strongly warned them not to go to Tongzhou. Taylor and Burdon thanked the man for his advice and stopped to consider their position.

'Well, what do you think,' asked Hudson.

Burdon paused and scratched his head. 'Has anything changed, Hudson? We knew Tongzhou was dangerous when we first decided to go there. One more warning doesn't make any difference. God will be with us.'

'Yes, that's what I think too. Let's go then.'

They continued on their way. As they went they recited Scripture to each other and sang:

The perils of the sea,
The perils of the land,
Should not dishearten thee;
Thy Lord is nigh at hand.

But should thy courage fail,
When tried and sore oppressed,
His promise shall avail,
And set thy soul at rest.

On the way they came across a small town and stopped to rest, but also took the opportunity to preach. As Hudson began speaking a crowd quickly assembled. He spoke in Mandarin and told them of the love of Christ and how He can heal the sinful heart. However, not all his listeners could understand Mandarin, but, to the surprise of the missionaries, one of their hearers began to repeat the message in the local dialect. When they had finished they distributed tracts and books and spoke to their translator, to reinforce the message in his mind. They then left, rejoicing in the responsiveness of the people in that town.

They suspected, though, that it was highly unlikely that the people of Tongzhou would respond as favourably. The wheelbarrow men remained with them until they arrived near the western gate of the city, then it was agreed that they would wait outside while Taylor and Burdon entered the city.

'We must take the books. Some of them, anyway!' said Hudson.

'Yes, we must.'

So, they lifted some bundles of books and tracts out of the wheelbarrows, hoisted them over their shoulders and began to walk to the gate. Two European men dressed in European-style clothing inevitably attracted attention. As they moved along the street leading to the western gate, dozens of people stared at them and shouted, 'Black devils! Black devils!'

At first that description puzzled the two visitors. 'Why are they calling us that?' asked Hudson of his companion. 'I'm used to being called a devil, but why *black* devils? We're not black.'

'I'm not sure,' said Burdon, as the two men continued walking. The people, including a few of the feared soldiers, kept their distance, but shouted their call again and again.

'Perhaps it's our clothes,' suggested Hudson.

The two westerners looked at each other. Both were dressed in dark clothing. Suddenly, 'Black devils' made sense.

Before they arrived at the gate a giant of a man confronted them. Drunk and aggressive, he stood in their way and made it clear to them that to go further would be dangerous. The two missionaries hesitated for a moment, but decided to walk around him. The massive soldier let out a roar and pounced upon Burdon, grabbing him by the shoulders. Before Hudson could decide on any action, another dozen fierce-looking men converged on them and herded them into the city.

As they were hustled through the gate, the giant let go of Burdon and grabbed hold of Hudson Taylor instead. He grabbed him by the collar and twisted it, choking him. Hudson gasped desperately for breath. Fortunately, the soldier soon released his grip, but then began to hit the missionary and violently forced him to the ground.

'Manacles! Manacles!' screamed the giant. 'Bring me some manacles for these black devils.'

A couple of his fellow-soldiers ran off to obey the command, but were unable to find any. When they returned, their mission unaccomplished, the giant let out a roar of disapproval and slapped one of them in anger.

Hudson, still on the ground, shivered. It was not because of cold, but fear. *Is this the end?* He wondered. *Lord, whatever happens may I glorify you.* He looked up at Burdon and said, 'Rejoicing that they were counted worthy to suffer in the cause of Christ.' Burdon, with a grim look on his face, nodded.

The soldiers then began to argue amongst themselves. It became clear that while the giant was the leader, not all of them liked or agreed with him. It was difficult to understand what they were saying, as they were all speaking at the same time. Yet Hudson clearly heard the word 'mandarin' and got the impression that some of them wanted to take the captives to the local magistrate. Yet others sounded, and looked, as though they favoured taking the law into their own hands and killing the unwanted visitors.

As they argued, Hudson pulled out a piece of red paper from his pocket and held it out towards the soldiers' leader. It was an identification document produced in Shanghai. The giant snatched the paper from Hudson, looked at it, as others in his band crowded around to see what it was.

As they examined it, again the two missionaries again heard the word 'mandarin.' The leader grunted, dragged Hudson violently to his feet and began to push him forward. Others were roughly pushing John Burdon in the same direction. The two missionaries assumed that they were headed for the mandarin's office. At least they could plead their case with him.

Eventually they arrived at the mandarin's residence, and the two exhausted missionaries were pushed violently into the courtyard. Their identification documents were taken to the mandarin. Now they had to wait, and the Chinese magistrate was in no hurry. As usual, a crowd gathered, and Burdon seized the opportunity and began to preach. The people listened, and Hudson handed out some tracts to them.

After what seemed an age a minor official appeared and reported that the mandarin, who was one of low rank, could not decide what to do with the two visitors, and said that they would have to be brought before a higher official. They were next taken to a senior mandarin. Fortunately, this mandarin had earlier served in Shanghai and was familiar with and sympathetic to Europeans.

'Why have you come to Tongzhou?' The mandarin's tone was stern, but not unkind.

'We have come to tell your people about God and His Son Jesus Christ,' said Hudson. 'We have books and tracts that tell you about how much He loves you. May I give you a book?' He held out a New Testament.

The mandarin signalled to a servant, who moved forward, took the Testament and gave it to the mandarin, who examined it closely.

'This book is the most precious book in the world,' said Hudson. 'It tells how the Lord Jesus Christ came to earth to die for us and to restore us to God. It tells how He died and how He rose again from the dead.'

The mandarin lifted his head a little from his looking at the New Testament. 'Rose from the dead?'

'Yes! It's all in that book. Jesus has power to forgive us our sins and give us eternal life, because He is God's Son and He died and rose from the dead.'

The mandarin was clearly interested. He signalled to some of the servants and they brought chairs for Taylor and Burdon, and later some refreshments. He began to fire questions at the two missionaries about this strange book, and they were only too glad to answer them.

After their discussion, the mandarin gave them permission to give tracts and books to people in the city and guaranteed them safe passage out of it. He even provided an escort and two sedan chairs for them to ride in to the centre of the city. When Taylor and Burdon had exhausted their supply of literature, they returned to where the two men were waiting with the wheelbarrows, and then went with them to their junk. A Chinese official accompanied them all the way to the river bank to make sure that they came to no harm. They arrived back in Shanghai 11 days after they had left it. It had been Hudson's longest tour so far, and he and his companion had distributed thousands of items of gospel literature.

In May he hired a junk and two boatmen to go on a journey that took more than three weeks. He travelled westward up the Yangtze and visited numerous towns, large and small. This was his furthest trip so far, reaching over 300 kilometres from Shanghai, and he took the gospel to some places where it had never been preached before.

The following month he went with John Burdon and William Parker south along the coast, visiting more towns, some of which had been devastated by pirates taking advantage of the lack of security during the war. For a while Hudson became separated from his two friends. He searched for them, but when he had almost given up hope of finding them they suddenly appeared. They travelled nearly 150 kilometres south to the major city of Ningpo, which was one of the five ports officially accessible to Europeans. They made some key contacts there and returned to Shanghai a little over two weeks after they had left it.

CHAPTER 9

THOSE HAPPY MONTHS

'Those happy months were an unspeakable joy and privilege to me' (Hudson Taylor).

In his first fifteen months in China Hudson Taylor had explored north, west and south of Shanghai. In that brief time, he had seen more of China than most other westerners stationed there. He also had come to recognise the importance and plausibility of moving further inland. His heart burned more than ever with the desire to take Christ to the Chinese people.

A thought had germinated in his mind leading mainly from his experiences in his travels. It was that wearing European clothing in China erected an unnecessary barrier between him and the people he hoped to reach. In Tongzhou he and John Burdon had been called 'black devils,' apparently because of their style of dress. This bothered him.

Should I adopt Chinese clothing? he asked himself. *Would that make reaching the Chinese people easier?*

Joseph Edkins of the LMS had already taken this step and Hudson advised the CES that he was also considering it. He told Pearse that this change was 'not to deceive' the people, 'but merely to avoid the astonishment that foreign clothes always produce, and the continual examination of which is very troublesome.' Indeed, as Hudson knew well, it was highly unlikely that the Chinese would be that easily deceived, at least not for long.

The subject refused to leave his mind. Later he thought, *I have already become adept at using chopsticks. So, if I eat like the Chinese, why shouldn't I dress like them?*

Hudson decided to approach Dr Medhurst to ask his opinion, as he was one of the most experienced and respected missionaries in the community.

'Dr Medhurst, I need some advice.'

'Yes, Hudson, what can I do for you?'

'Well, it's about wearing European clothes.' He looked down at his suit and shirt. 'They seem to present a barrier between us and the Chinese. I'm considering adopting Chinese clothing. What do you think?'

Medhurst thought for a moment. 'Well, Hudson, I have done that on occasions when I've travelled inland. As you know, the further you move into China, the fewer people are familiar with Europeans and our style of dress. It seemed to me safer to do that. And, as you say, less of a barrier.'

'But I'm thinking of doing so all the time.'

Medhurst paused again. 'I see no harm in it. Indeed, Mr Edkins seems to wear Chinese clothing more now than British cloth, so you won't be alone.'

Hudson smiled. 'Yes, I've noticed.'

If Hudson's mind had not previously been made up, it certainly was now. He would take this step. He made some enquiries and was soon kitted out in Chinese garb.

He also decided to wear a pigtail, a black one. But his hair was a reddish colour, so he needed to dye it. He proposed to use ammonia in this process, a half-full bottle of which he already had.

So, a day or two later, he picked up the bottle and began to ease off the stopper. Suddenly, it exploded. The stopper flew past his ear and ammonia sprayed all over his face and into his eyes. The pain was excruciating. He screamed in agony. He rushed blindly to a nearby water tub and dipped his face into it.

He lifted his head out of the water, gasped and shouted, 'Get Dr Parker. Get Dr Parker, quick.'

A Chinese servant rushed into the room, saw Hudson Taylor was in trouble and raced off to get Dr Parker.

Parker soon arrived. 'What's wrong? What's happened?'

'Help me, Dr Parker. It's ammonia.'

Parker needed no more telling. The powerful, pungent smell pervaded the room and Hudson's distress was evident. The doctor hastened to the young man's side and examined his face and eyes, and rinsed them again with clean water. He then bandaged Hudson's eyes, gave him a sedative and put him to bed.

As he lay there Hudson thought, *Thank God I was wearing my spectacles, or it would have been worse.*

A few days later he was up and about, with little trace of the incident, other than a redness about the face and a runny nose. But he had to wait a little longer for his black pigtail.

***

Late in 1855 William Chalmers Burns arrived in Shanghai. He had previously been stationed in Amoy in the south-east, had returned to Britain and had just arrived back in China. Burns was a Presbyterian evangelist, who had been a major figure in a revival in Scotland in 1839. He was originally sent as a missionary to China by the English Presbyterian Mission in 1847. Sometime after his arrival in Amoy, Burns had saved the lives of a number of Chinese men, when hundreds had been attacked, injured and dumped in the sea by the Manchus. This had made him very popular amongst the Chinese throughout that region.

Hudson Taylor was 17 years younger than Burns and far less experienced in mission work, yet he and Burns shared a great passion for taking the gospel to the Chinese. They quickly formed a friendship, even for a time a partnership. Taylor later called Burns 'this beloved and honoured servant of God.'

They left Shanghai together on 17 December 1855, each in his own boat, with two boatmen and two servants for company, along with a Chinese Christian teacher named Song. It was also planned that Guihua and Tsien would meet up with them later. Taylor was dressed in Chinese attire, Burns in European.

Their main target city on this trip was to be Wuzhen towards the west, which was also known as Black Town. Its reputation was as black as its nickname. They also intended to minister in other towns along the way a little to the south and then to the west. They were not taking an easy path.

When they reached the first town they discussed their strategy.

'How should we approach this, Hudson?'

'I usually start in the town centre and if possible move out from there.'

'What happens?'

'Well, it varies. Often you get a big crowd, but sometimes that's a disadvantage. It gets noisy and can even become violent.' Hudson paused. 'What do you think?'

'I wonder if it would be better to start on the fringe of the town and when at least some of the people have become used to us move to the centre. I have tried that and it usually works well. Every place is different, of course.'

Hudson stroked his beard as he thought. 'Yes, that makes sense. Let's try that.'

Their regular practice from then was that when docked near a town they started their day with prayer and left their boats at about 9 a.m., carrying a stool and bags of literature. When they reached a suitable spot, usually on the fringe of the town, one would climb on the stool and preach, while the other knelt nearby in prayer. Usually a crowd gathered, and after about 20 minutes the two men swapped places. They continued this for an hour or more. Then they handed out leaflets and New Testaments and spoke individually to those who seemed especially interested.

They returned to their boats for lunch, followed by more prayer, and then went out and found another preaching spot closer to the centre of the town. In the evenings, they usually visited tea-shops and talked with the customers, placing Scriptures in their hands.

Hudson soon discovered that some of the methods William Burns used were more aggressive than his own. When they reached the town of Nanxun, which was near the Great Lake to the west of Shanghai, they took turns in preaching but Hudson was unwell and soon had to stop and rest.

While there they heard about a notorious encampment just outside the town and, on the insistence of Burns, paid the camp a visit. When they arrived, they discovered a stage surrounded by thousands of people, mainly men, with some sheds, a brothel and gambling booths nearby. Actors played out their roles in a drama and musicians played their instruments, while prostitutes plied their trade.

'This is Satan's camp,' said Burns.

'Yes, but what can we do?' said Hudson, hesitantly.

'Watch me, and I'll show you what we can do.'

With that Burns marched forward, climbed on to the stage and began to preach. Hudson nervously moved forward in support, but stayed at the foot of the stairs.

With the unexpected appearance of Burns the actors stopped. The crowd became silent. Burns continued to have his say, warning the people about the sinfulness of their ways and the judgement of God. The message that Burns preached and the clothing he wore were both strange to these people, and they quickly realised that he was European.

Suddenly the crowd erupted into an explosion of protest. Two of the actors grabbed hold of Burns and led him off the stage. Perhaps strangely, they did so without undue violence. They then led him outside the camp and told him to go and not come back. He went and Hudson followed.

The two missionaries began to retreat to their boat.

'Was that too foolhardy, do you think?' asked Hudson when they could no longer hear the noise from the encampment.

'Yes, maybe!' Burns ran his fingers through his hair in agitation. 'But we have to go back. Those people will die and go to hell without Christ. We have to go back.'

'Yes! Yes, I agree. But perhaps we should moderate our tactics.'

'I suppose so,' said Burns.

The next day they returned to the outskirts of the camp and took it in turns to preach from a ladder. Some listened, but it was not long before they were once more escorted away. It seemed that they were bad for business.

They decided not to return to the camp at that time, and in the following days they made return visits to the town of Nanxun. They carried out their now usual policy of preaching in the outskirts first and then moving to the centre. In that town they attracted attention and some sympathy. They also discovered that some residents in the city had heard about their adventures in the encampment and strongly approved of their actions, encouraging them to go back.

Taylor and Burns returned to their boat to pray and discuss their next step. They prayed for some time, and soon after nightfall they went to bed.

In the morning they discussed what to do. 'Well, do we go back to the camp?' asked Hudson.

'We must.'

'It's dangerous.'

'I know, but God will be with us.'

'Yes, He will,' said Hudson. 'But I have a suggestion.'

'What's that?'

'You let me do the preaching. At least at first!'

'Why?' Burns responded, sounding a little offended.

'You see, I wear Chinese clothing. That might make them more ready to listen. European clothing makes it too obvious that we are foreigners. "Black devils!" you see.'

Burns thought for a moment. 'Yes, you have a point.' He paused once more. Hudson's comments made good sense. 'Right! Let's go. You preach and I'll stay in the background unless things get too hot.'

So, they went to the camp. Hudson entered the camp without any trouble, while his companion remained on the outskirts, but close enough to see the stage. No one seemed to realise that Hudson was a foreigner. He reached the stage, climbed the stairs and began to lift his voice above the actors. He ordered them to stop. The players stared at him in confused silence. At first many in the crowd seemed to assume that he was another actor and that it was all part of the drama, but it soon became clear to them that his message had nothing to do with the play.

'I have a message for you all from the God of heaven,' he cried out. 'Jesus Christ came into this world to save sinners,'

All eyes seemed to be on him, so he made the most of his opportunity.

'Jesus is the Son of God, and he died to save you from your sins.' His voice sounded out eerily in the strange quiet. 'He can save you. He can give you eternal life.'

By this time some of the minders beside the stage had realised that something was wrong and that this strange man had no right to be on the platform. They rushed up the stairs, grabbed hold of Hudson and dragged him off the stage. They gave him a push, but did not take him outside the camp.

Hudson was unhurt and returned to where Burns stood. 'I'll give it another try,' Hudson told him. 'But in a less conspicuous spot.'

Burns nodded and gave a grim smile.

Hudson began to meander about the camp looking for a good preaching place. Burns followed him, but kept his distance. Hudson saw a prostitute rise from a stool and go off with a man, so he grabbed the stool, moved it to a convenient position and stood on it. Once more his message was simple but confronting.

He pointed in the direction the prostitute was taking and said to his male audience 'Would you allow your daughters to do that? Would you allow your daughters to carry out this wicked trade? Then why use other men's daughters in this way?'

Surprisingly the men listened, or at least some of them did, for Taylor and Burns heard some in the crowd repeating the questions that Hudson had asked. There was plenty of noise coming from the area surrounding the stage, but those from the crowd that had assembled around the two missionaries were strangely quiet.

Hudson began to preach, while his companion gave out testaments and tracts. The literature was grabbed with enthusiasm and some in the crowd stayed to listen. They seemed to think it a strange message from a strange man. Some looked at the booklets that they had been given, while others examined William's clothing, grabbing it and pulling it.

When the two men returned to their boat late that afternoon, elated by the day's events, Burns raised the issue of dress once more.

'Hudson, this business of Chinese clothes: Do you think that they really make the Chinese accept you more readily?'

Hudson thought for a moment. 'Well, yes, I do. I don't believe it leads them to think I am Chinese; except perhaps at first glance. But I do think it removes a barrier. I've been invited into more homes since I adopted Chinese dress.'

'I see.'

'Are you thinking of wearing them too?'

'Aye, I am. Might be more comfortable in summer too.'

Hudson laughed. 'Even in winter, surprising as it may seem.'

'That's good. I need some protection from this cold.'

In fact, the padded jacket with the all-covering gown were good protection against the elements.

The next day they returned to the town of Nanxun. On this occasion they were treated rather differently, for it was clear that news of what they had done in the encampment had reached the town. People stared at them. When they stood up to preach, people listened. One man followed them from preaching spot to preaching spot and asked them a host of questions about the Christian faith. William and Hudson were only too glad to answer them, give him a New Testament and point him to Christ.

While in Nanxun William Burns went shopping. He purchased Chinese clothing, put it on and did not regret his decision.

They remained near Nanxun into the new year, preaching frequently in the town. Each evening when they returned to their boat they were followed by men and women keen to know more about the Christian faith. Taylor and Burns were just as keen to tell them.

On January 8, they moved on to Wuzhen, a little further to the east. Taylor later said, 'The people seemed much surprised' by their arrival; their Chinese clothes presumably had not hidden their identity. Hudson thought they may have been the first Europeans in the city. On the first morning they preached in a temple dedicated to the God of War, then later moved to a site where some homes had been destroyed by fire. In the afternoon they preached again on the fire-devastated site, and visited a tea shop in the evening accompanied by Tsien and another Chinese helper Kuei-hua before returning to their boat. Kuei-hua had been Hudson's servant and had been converted as a result of the Englishman's witness and lifestyle.

Two days later Tsien and Kuei-hua went into the town early to distribute tracts and later joined Taylor and Burns in a return to the burnt-out site to preach in two pairs. They then returned to the boats. On the bank a crowd had assembled, each person eager to speak with the missionaries. Taylor and Burns answered their questions as best they could, helped by their Chinese companions, and then boarded Hudson's boat to have lunch. However, this was the calm before the storm.

Bang! Thump! It was something crashing on the roof. They rushed up on deck to see what was happening and were confronted by five aggressive-looking men on the bank, flinging clods of frozen earth at their boat.

As the missionaries and their Chinese colleagues appeared on deck a roar went up from the attackers. 'Kill the foreign devils! Kill the foreign devils!' More clods of earth soared through the air and landed on the vessel. The four Christians ducked and weaved to avoid the missiles. They managed to escape injury, but their boat was less fortunate and took a battering.

While this was happening, another houseboat passed by. Its occupants watched events closely.

'Stop! Stop!' It was Tsien calling to the people on the other boat. 'Come close and let me board.'

The men on the other boat looked at Tsien, the boat on which he stood and the aggressors on the bank. They then looked at each other, not quite sure what to do. Fortunately, they soon decided it was safe to agree to Tsien's request and came close enough for him to board.

'Quick! Quick! Put me off further along the bank,' Tsien said, with a host of emphatic gestures.

The boatmen went a short distance down the canal, and let Tsien off. The courageous Chinaman then stood on the bank waving some tracts he had taken from the supply on board the missionary boat.

The aggressors stopped their attack and looked at Tsien, who was still waving the tracts. They looked at each other and then began to move quickly to where Tsien stood.

'This looks dangerous,' said Hudson nervously. 'What can we do?'

'Whatever we do I think we will be too late,' responded Burns.

The five men reached where Tsien bravely stood. He held out the tracts to them. They took them, stood for a while and slowly wandered off examining their treasures.

Within minutes Tsien returned to the boat.

'What was that all about?' a much-relieved Hudson Taylor asked Tsien.

'They thought they'd been unfairly treated in the literature distribution. They were just showing their displeasure. Now they've got what they wanted.'

The four Christians finished their meal, and went back on deck. To their surprise a large crowd had assembled, attracted by the news of the earlier disturbance.

'It looks like we have a congregation,' said Burns.

'Yes, it does. And a big one too!'

So, they stepped down from the boat and took their opportunity, preaching to the assembled throng. The people listened attentively and in silence. When the missionaries had finished, they distributed tracts and testaments.

After the crowd had dispersed Taylor and Burns examined the damages to the boat. Fortunately, they were not major and so the trip would not have to be cut short. The next day they repaired the boat.

A shopkeeper named Yao visited them on that day. He had received gospel portions from them when they had first arrived in Wuzhen and he wanted to know more, but agreed that it was best to come back when the missionaries had made their repairs. The next day he returned and gave Hudson a note written partly in biblical language, requesting a New Testament and more literature. It was clear that Yao had immersed himself in the gospel message and had been deeply moved by it.

Hudson and his companions were stunned at how quickly the man had come to understand the message of Jesus Christ. They gave him a New Testament and other literature and spoke at length with him.

Because their work was progressing favourably in Wuzhen, they decided to stay a few more days. They carried on preaching during the day and visiting the tea-rooms in the evening. One night they returned to their boats and found one of their boatmen in a rather agitated state. They were carrying a lit lantern, but, without saying anything, the boatman grabbed hold of it and extinguished the candle. Hudson lit it again, but the boatman grabbed the candle and threw it into the canal.

'What's wrong? What are you afraid of?' asked Hudson.

The boatman remained silent. He seemed too afraid to speak.

'Tell us, man. What's happened?' It was Burns this time.

The boatman was clearly involved in an intense inner struggle. Should he tell, or shouldn't he? At last the words burst forth in rapid fire. 'A man came. He is one of band of smugglers. Lots of them! They want money and opium. They all come tomorrow.'

The boatman's evident fear left Taylor and Burns in no doubt that they were in real danger. They looked for the other boatman, and when they found him he was even more terrified than his companion. Travelling at night was not usually considered a wise option, but they decided that this was what they should do. They calmed the boatmen down, made sure all their possessions were on board the two boats and rowed away.

When they had moved well away from that site, they moored the boats again and gathered for prayer. They read from the ninety-first Psalm.

He that dwelleth in the secret place of the most High
Shall abide under the shadow of the Almighty.
I will say to the Lord, He is my refuge and my fortress;
My God, in Him will I trust.
Surely He shall deliver thee...

And He did deliver them. The smugglers did not find them.

CHAPTER 10

AN INESTIMABLE PRIZE

'A good wife – one who would sympathise with me and assist me – would be an inestimable prize' (Hudson Taylor).

During 1855 on his trip to Wuzhen with William Burns, Hudson Taylor had mused about the possibility of having 'a helpmate and fellow-labourer' to share his joys and sorrows. It was, at that stage, only a dream.

In his teens he had fallen in love with a friend of his sister's, a young music teacher named Marianne Vaughan, his 'dear Miss V.' She also loved him. But by that time he was determined to become a missionary to China and this presented a barrier. She kept asking him 'Must you go to China?' He knew that he must, but it was a struggle for him to remain firm on that commitment. That struggle went on for many months. At one point she seemed to have relented on the China issue and they became engaged. However, the engagement was eventually broken, due to pressure from her father, and they went their separate ways. It was a difficult period for each of them.

Hudson later became fond of another young lady named Elizabeth Sissons, who was in the circle of friends that included Hudson's sister, Amelia, and Marianne Vaughan. Elizabeth's father, after some hesitation, permitted them to correspond, both while Hudson was in London and later when he was in Shanghai. Hudson even sent her gifts from China, despite his limited finances.

Loneliness hit him hard in China, and he felt a deep need of a wife to love. In one letter to his sister Amelia he said that he had some flowers in his room, to which he had given names. Two he named after Amelia and Louisa, his other sister, and, he added, 'what I have called a third is no matter of yours.' But it was presumably Elizabeth.

He proposed marriage to her, but communicating between China and England was a slow, frustrating process. When a response eventually came from Mr Sissons, the answer was neither yes nor no, which left Hudson confused and even more frustrated. Then the bombshell came: a letter from Elizabeth saying that 'she feared' that she did not love him. He told his mother in a letter that he was 'quite knocked down' by this news. That was probably an understatement. Yet she had not actually said no to the proposal, but, he thought, *Surely, that must follow*.

After much more thought and prayer, he became concerned that he was making Elizabeth an idol, so he decided to resign himself to God's will, whatever that might be. Another letter arrived from Elizabeth. It said 'No' to his proposal.

He wrote to Amelia clearly expressing his feelings. 'Had this come a month ago,' he told her, 'I think it would have been more than I could have borne, but I have been prepared for it, and was not at all surprised.'

Being faithful to what one believes is God's call is not always easy. Temptations abound, and even legitimate pathways can lead to lesser destinations. But unexpectedly Hudson saw light at the end of this dark tunnel, and that light was not shining from England but from China. That light was Maria Dyer.

Samuel Dyer, Maria's father, was a law student who went to Asia as a missionary for the LMS in 1827 and served in Penang and Malacca (in what is today Malaysia) and Singapore. He was an expert linguist. He married Maria Tarn, who was the daughter of a director of the LMS. They had five children, three of whom lived to adulthood: Samuel Jr, Burella (Ellie) and Maria Jane. Samuel Sr died in 1843 and his wife died three years later.

Upon the death of Mrs Dyer, Maria and her brother and sister went to England to live with their mother's relatives. However, Maria and Ellie had spent most of their lives in Asia, so it was no surprise that, while still teenagers, they responded to a call to serve in China. And, having grown up in China, they spoke Chinese fluently.

They went to Ningpo, one of the five access ports, and taught in a school for girls run by the formidable Mary Ann Aldersey, a friend of the late Mrs Dyer. It was uncommon at that time to send unmarried women to China as missionaries, but the 'domineering and remarkable' Mary Aldersey had paved the way for others to follow. Both Europeans and Chinese held Miss Aldersey in awe. Some of the Chinese even feared that she had magical powers, and, for some strange reason, they thought she could cause earthquakes. She also taught blind girls to read at her school, which mystified many of the local people.

In the middle of August 1856, Hudson Taylor went to Ningpo and spent about six weeks there. It was increasingly thought amongst the missionary community that Ningpo was a key city for the spread of the gospel in China, though Chinese opposition to European settlement there was growing. Taylor called Ningpo 'one of the most ancient and influential cities on the coast of China.'

William Parker and his family had already moved to Ningpo from Shanghai. The Parkers dined weekly with Mary Aldersey and the Dyer sisters. When Hudson was in Ningpo he went visiting with the Parkers and met Ellie and Maria.

Later that year Maria visited some Chinese homes with Mary Jones, a recently arrived CES missionary. When they had finished they took tea together at Mary's home. Hudson Taylor also just happened to be present on this occasion, and afterwards he escorted the attractive, dark-haired Maria home. However, at that stage visions of Elizabeth

Sissons still buzzed through his brain, so this occurrence, for him, was little more than an increase of his awareness of Maria. Yet she already felt the first flicker of love for the handsome Hudson Taylor.

In January 1857 Maria made an entry in her diary that read, 'Mr. Kloekers and Mr. Taylor called' for a prayer meeting. Little by little Hudson Taylor and Maria Dyer were getting to know each other. His thoughts about Elizabeth became fewer, while his thoughts about the sweet-natured Maria increased. Soon after that Maria recorded, 'I had some little reason, perhaps, to think that he might be interested in me.' However, she wondered if she might be imagining it. Yet she was hopeful that he would show increased interest in her.

Chinese opposition to Europeans in Ningpo became more and more apparent and the situation began to look very dangerous. Therefore, most of the children and the women missionaries, though not Maria, were sent to Shanghai, while most of the men remained behind. Hudson Taylor and John Jones, the husband of Mary, were appointed to escort the women to their destination. Maria went down to the harbour to see them off.

Whether the old saying 'Absence makes the heart go fonder' is true or not may be debated, but as Hudson spent time away from Maria in another city he seemed to think more about her. But he had previously fallen in love with Marianne, and had been disappointed. He had fallen in love with Elizabeth, and again had known great disappointment. These experiences made him cautious. However, his feelings for Maria deepened. She seemed to be forever in his mind.

On 21 March Hudson wrote a letter to Maria, making a hesitant proposal of marriage. Fearing a possible rejection, he asked her not to respond hastily. Still unsure of his feelings and his prospects, he waited for another two days before he posted it. Then it took two weeks to reach her in Ningpo. When she received it, she read it with considerable excitement and enthusiasm. God, it seems, was answering her wavering prayers.

However, she was only 20 and was too young to get married without the permission of her guardian, an uncle in England. In addition, she also had a strict chaperone in Miss Aldersey, who did not wholly approve of Hudson Taylor.

Maria approached Mary Aldersey rather nervously, clutching the letter in her hand.

'Miss Aldersey, I have something to tell you. And I need your help.'

'What is it, my girl?'

Maria held up the letter. 'Hudson Taylor has asked me to marry him.'

'Has he, indeed? And why would you want to marry him?' the teacher said with a scowl.

'But I do, Miss Aldersey. I do. And I believe it is God's will that I do.'

'Do you now? And what do you know about this man?'

'I know he is a godly man and intent on taking the gospel to the Chinese. And I believe that he loves me.'

'Love! Hmmm! He's been writing to you then?'

'Yes.'

'I didn't give him permission. How old are you? Twenty?'

'Yes.'

'You are not of age. You can't get married without the permission of your guardian, Mr Tarn, in England.'

There was silence for a moment as both considered the matter. Then Maria said, 'Miss Aldersey, will you write to him for me. I'm sure uncle William will give his permission.'

Aldersey thought for a moment. 'Yes, I'll write, but I'll ask him to find out more about this Hudson Taylor.'

Maria was disappointed by Miss Aldersey's response but not

surprised. Miss Aldersey wrote her letter. Back in England William Tarn was ill, but when he received this letter he began to investigate the background of Hudson Taylor.

Meanwhile Maria was in a most difficult situation. She had received a proposal of marriage from a fine Christian man, which she wanted to accept, but was not allowed to do so.

She sent Hudson a reply that probably pleased nobody. When Hudson received it, he knew it was from her and he opened it with trembling hands and great hope. It began with staunch Victorian formality. 'Dear Sir,' she wrote, 'I have to acknowledge receipt of a letter from you dated March 21st.' She then thanked him for 'the kind Christian spirit that breathed throughout' his letter, and continued, 'I have made the subject of your letter a matter of earnest prayer to God, and have desired, I think sincerely, only to know His will, and to act in accordance with it. And although it does indeed give me no pleasure to cause you pain, I must answer your letter as appears to me to be according to God's direction. And it certainly appears to me to be my duty to decline your proposals.'

Hudson read that sentence again and again: 'it certainly appears to be my duty to decline your proposals.' Decline your proposals? He was stunned. Hudson by this time had received a rejection from Marianne Vaughan, another from Elizabeth Sissons, and now a third from Maria Dyer. *What's wrong with me?* he wondered.

He read on and learned that Maria had shown his letter to her sister and Miss Aldersey, but he thought nothing of it at the time. Then Maria continued, 'Before I close this letter, I shall take an opportunity of burning yours as you desired me.' He had said that, so he could not complain on that score, but the thought of her burning a letter that had cost him so much and held out such hopes hurt him deeply.

But she went further. 'I regard you, dear Sir, as a Brother in Jesus, and hope ever to bear towards you those feelings which Disciples are commanded to bear towards one another. But ask me not for more. I request you not to refer to the subject again as I shall be obliged to return you the same answer.'

Hudson was distraught. He did not know the circumstances behind the letter, for they were at best only hinted at, and the letter sounded final. There appeared to be no hope. There was not even a mention of the fact that as she was not yet twenty-one she was unable to marry without the permission of her guardian. And she had said, 'I request you not to refer to the subject again.'

Those words burned in his mind and on his heart. He poured out his struggle to God in prayer, but it was only later that he suspected that there was more hope behind that letter than was apparent in the mere words.

But other matters rose to the forefront of his mind. His association with the CES had gone from bad to worse. He had never been completely comfortable with the missionary organisation that sent him to China and had given him little support of any kind, and while the financial aspect was at least partly caused by economic problems in Britain, encouragement had also been lacking. On May 29 Hudson sent George Pearse a letter of resignation. This meant that he now had no guarantee of receiving any money, except from the God who provides. Strikingly, these troubles had thrown him more into the arms of God. There he could find comfort in prayer.

Money did come too, although not in plentiful supply. George Müller of Bristol sent him £40 later in the year, with a message of encouragement. Another windfall, modest but regular, was to come.

Soon after Taylor had resigned from the CES, John and Mary Jones did likewise. At this time, Hudson was forming a close friendship with the Joneses and he was inspired by their great dedication and faith.

The work of taking the gospel to the Chinese had to continue, with or without the support of a mission agency and with or without the support of a loving wife. Later in the year the troubles in Ningpo had calmed down, so he returned there. But he knew that he would inevitably meet Maria again and be faced with the problem of how to relate to her.

On his return to Ningpo he, surprisingly, rarely bumped into Maria. Instead he found himself repeatedly confronted by Miss Aldersey. It gradually dawned upon him that she was 'where the difficulty lay,' so Hudson approached her and raised the subject of his relationship with Maria.

'Young man,' she said, 'your letter was most improper. You should have approached Miss Dyer through me, not directly. It was *most* improper.'

'Are you her guardian then?'

'Well, no. But her guardian is in England, so I act on his behalf. Her interests are very much my concern. And I don't think it is in her interests to marry you, young man.'

Miss Aldersey's words were delivered with considerable force, causing Hudson to take a literal backward step. But that was the only backward step he was prepared to take.

'But why? What do you have against me?'

'Young man, I don't have to tell you. That is between me and Miss Dyer. And her guardian!'

The debate continued, but Hudson soon realised that he would never persuade her to change her mind. However, this encounter, troubling though it had been, gave him great hope. It was now clear that Maria had said no to him because Miss Aldersey would not let her say yes.

If Miss Aldersey's opposition seems rather irrational, it must be realised that at this time Hudson Taylor was a man of little obvious ability and limited prospects. In addition, she was not the only person in Ningpo who thought Hudson Taylor an unworthy suitor.

These troubles went on and on. However, Hudson and Maria did meet on a few occasions, sometimes secretly, and it became clear to him that she was more than happy for him to refer to the subject of marriage once more. So he did.

In December Maria received a letter from Mrs Tarn in England saying that she and her husband had no objection to them marrying. Mr Tarn had carried out some investigations into the character of Hudson Taylor and was duly satisfied. However, the letter added that she must wait until she was 21.

But the pages of the calendar were quickly turning over. On January 16, 1858 Maria Dyer became 21. She was now legally free to make her own choices, so she was able to marry. Hudson was over the moon with happiness. As he expressed at that time, 'She is a treasure; she is all I desire.' A mere four days later Hudson Taylor and Maria Dyer were married.

The American Consul lent the Taylors his sedan chair for the wedding. It was a pretty chair, Hudson thought, but made 'prettier' by the bride it carried. She wore a 'simple grey silk gown' and a veil. The text the minister spoke from at their wedding was 'Keep yourselves from idols.' That was appropriate to Hudson and Maria from two perspectives. They were surrounded by idols in the midst of a mainly Buddhist community and there was always the danger that they would make idols of each other.

What Hudson only found out just before the wedding was that Maria would be the recipient of a family legacy worth about £40 a year. That would not solve all their financial problems, but it would be a great help.

A week after the wedding Hudson wrote, 'We are so happy! The Lord Himself has turned our sorrow into joy, giving us "the garment of praise for the spirit of heaviness."'

CHAPTER 11

NINGPO

'If I had a thousand pounds China should have it—if I had a thousand lives, China should have them. No! Not China, but Christ. Can we do too much for Him? Can we do enough for such a precious Saviour?' (Hudson Taylor to his sister Amelia).

After their honeymoon Hudson and Maria settled in a village just outside Ningpo, but later moved into Ningpo, as it was better as a centre for their activities. Then Maria caught typhoid fever. Hudson was distraught. With his medical training, he knew that typhoid could kill, and for a while it seemed to him as though he would lose his beloved wife. For so long he had desired and prayed for a wife; for so long he had prayed that Maria would be his, and now it seemed as if she could be snatched away from him. He agonised with God in prayer.

Mercifully, by this time William Parker had established a hospital in Ningpo. Gradually Maria began to improve. Then Hudson caught the disease. They were nursed by the Parkers and other missionaries, and slowly recovered, but they were not really well until April, three months after their wedding.

Hudson Taylor was now married, free from any ties to a mission organisation and in reasonable health. It was a good time to plan. The primary problems facing them, and, indeed, all those concerned with taking the gospel of Christ to the Chinese, were the size of the country, the enormous population, the limited impact Christianity had made thus far in that land, and the scarcity of Christian workers. The situation demanded a larger number of dedicated missionaries and an energetic movement inland, away from the five treaty ports. But it also demanded something even more important: determined Chinese Christians taking the gospel to their own people. However, all of this could not be done in a moment. It would take time and it would take planning.

At that time, amidst the nearly 400 million Chinese there were only about 90 Protestant missionaries in China, plus 50 Chinese preachers. Evangelising the whole of China seemed impossible. But Hudson Taylor and others believed that it could be done.

One step towards this goal was completely out of the hands of the missionaries, and opposed by most if not all of them. It was the Second Opium War (1856-60), in which the British and French attacked China, partly so they could continue the trade in opium. Wicked though this was, it resulted in ten more Chinese ports being opened to European traders and missionaries. Despite continued Chinese reluctance to allow missionaries into the interior, further discussions between the various parties made this possible under certain conditions.

Hudson was by this time so proficient in various Chinese tongues and so respected that he was often asked to interpret for the Consul and in court cases.

In the second half of 1858 Hudson sent two letters to the *Gleaner*, encouraging more Christians to volunteer for missionary service. In them he appealed for prayer 'that many labourers may be raised up, both here and in other lands, to preach Christ and him crucified to the untold millions of this now opened land.' He also said, 'And oh, will not the Church at home awake herself, and send out many to publish the glad tidings.'

The Taylors meanwhile worked with John and Mary Jones in Ningpo in a mission church that they established in Bridge Street in the south-west of the city. Identifiable results were scarce at first. However, one evening Hudson had just finished preaching the gospel of Christ, when a middle-aged Chinaman stood up. As he did, the other Chinese became silent, which suggested he was a man of some importance.

He addressed them, speaking with deep emotion. 'I have long sought for the truth,' he said, 'as my fathers did before me. But I've never found it. I've travelled far and near without discovering it. I have found no rest in Confucianism, Buddhism or Taoism.' His voice then rose in pitch. 'But I do find rest in what I have heard tonight. I am now a believer in Jesus Christ.'

A gasp went around the room. The man was a leading figure in a group of Buddhists in the city, and his confession of belief in Christ made a major impact upon all who heard about it. By the end of August 1858 they had about six converts. While this was a small number it was, at least, a base upon which to build.

In April that year Hudson had sent a letter to his mother, telling her that she should 'expect a Christmas box that will transform you into a Grandmother.' Unfortunately, that Christmas box came two months prematurely, when that October Maria gave birth to a baby. Sadly, the child died soon after.

Maria and Hudson felt the pain deeply. It was heartbreaking. In England and in China the death of infants in these circumstances and others was common, but that did not make it any easier to bear.

In 1859 Christian work in Ningpo moved ahead with greater success. Hudson wrote a letter to George Pearse, with whom he still enjoyed a good relationship, telling him that 'the work here is most cheering at present. Our Baptist friends here have 7 most interesting young men candidates for baptism. Our Presbyterian friends admitted no less than 12 (six of each sex) into the church last Lord's Day but one,' and about five were received into the Anglican Church. Each church in the city seemed to be able to report carrying out baptisms of Chinese people.

The Taylors and the Joneses also saw conversions and baptisms at their Bridge Street mission. And the relationship between the various denominations and missions was friendly and cooperative overall. However, this was not going on in a peaceful environment: Rebellion and the resulting war were continuing in the towns around them.

One Sunday in May, Hudson was, as usual, involved in a variety of activities at his church. That evening some Chinese men dragged into the church a man who had tried to commit suicide by overdosing on opium. He was in a terrible state, raving incoherently and struggling to escape the grip of the men who held him. Suddenly he escaped their clutch and tried to get away, but his movements were slow and he was soon recaptured. The men brought him to Hudson.

'Is it opium?' Hudson asked, strongly suspecting the likely answer.

'Yes,' said one. 'A lot! He's trying to kill himself.'

'Keep hold of him. I'll get my medical bag.'

Hudson rushed off and came back with the bag. 'I am going to administer an emetic,' he told the man's companions. 'I hope that will help. Hold him please.'

The men held their friend, while he struggled vainly. Hudson administered the dose, and soon the man gave up fighting and relaxed.

'Take him into the house,' said Hudson.

The men did so, and, following Hudson's instructions, they placed the drugged man on a bed.

'We'll look after him. Come back in the morning if you wish.'

The Chinese men bowed and left.

'What's happening?' It was Maria.

'It seems we have a lodger for the night,' said Hudson. 'A man tried to commit suicide and was brought to us by his friends. He's in a bit of a mess. Opium! He's in the guest room.'

'Oh! Is there anything I can do?'

'Not at the moment. I'll sit with him for a while and see what happens. You go to bed.'

Hudson returned to the room in which they had placed the man. He was already in a drugged sleep. Hudson sat with him until about two in the morning and then he joined Maria in bed.

The next morning Hudson looked in on the man, but he was still asleep. The Taylors had breakfast. As they ate, the man appeared. He was still drowsy and was rather unsteady on his feet.

'Sit down,' said Hudson. 'Would you like something to eat?'

The man walked to the table with an unsteady gait and sat down. He looked at the food on the table but ate nothing.

There was silence for a while and then the man said, 'You helped me last night, didn't you? You saved my life.'

'I did what I believe the Lord Jesus Christ would have done.'

The man stared blankly at Hudson.

'When you've recovered I will tell you about Him.'

Once more the man stared at Hudson blankly.

'You are still worn out. If you wish, you may go back to your room and sleep more. You are our guest.'

'You may stay as long as you like,' said Maria.

The man stood shakily and made his way back to the room, with Hudson escorting him.

The visitor stayed a few days and the Taylors cared for him while he recovered. They talked to him about Jesus and salvation through Him, but, while he showed interest, there was no significant response. Soon the man left. But the seed had been planted.

Chinese Christians were now often involved in evangelism, both planned and informal. Feng Nenggui, a basket-weaver, had become a Christian through the Bridge Street mission, but he was dismissed from his employment because he refused to work on Sundays. Word travelled about his stand for Christ, and no one else would employ him. However, he began to make and sell some baskets working on his own.

Feng also began to frequent the tea shops and speak about Christ. One day a woman invited him into her home and asked him to make some incense baskets for her. Because he was now a Christian he refused to do it. The woman was not pleased.

Also in the house that day was a strongly-built Chinaman up on a ladder, painting the interior of the house. This was Wang Lea-djun. He heard the conversation and was shocked and puzzled by what Feng had said. Yet, it seemed connected to an earlier experience that he had had. Wang had previously been a farmer in an outlying area, but had heard a mysterious voice telling him to go to Ningpo, where he would hear about a religion that would give him peace. He thought peace sounded very attractive in a world of war, so he went to Ningpo and set himself up as a painter and decorator to pay his way.

Wang wondered, *Could the words of this strange basket weaver be the key to this religion, this peace?* So, he approached Feng and asked him about his beliefs. Feng invited Wang to his home and there he stayed. Feng shared the gospel with his new friend, pointing out verses from the New Testament, and after considerable discussion Wang trusted Christ for salvation.

Sunday July 1, 1859, was a very hot day in Ningpo. The temperature soared above 40° C. John Jones was taking the service in the stifling heat at Bridge Street Church. But Hudson Taylor, Mary Jones and, especially, Maria Taylor had something else to deal with that day. Maria was about to give birth. After the tragic loss of their first child, the Taylors were, understandably, a little nervous, but Grace Dyer Taylor came into the world in good health.

Late one afternoon towards the end of that August there was a knock on the Taylors' door. When Maria opened it, an agitated Chinese servant greeted her.

'Mr Taylor, come quick, please. Mrs Parker very sick.'

'At the hospital?'

'No! At home! Mr Taylor, come quick.'

Maria called Hudson, told him the news and he hurried to the Parkers' home. When he arrived he found an ashen-faced William Parker.

'What's wrong?' Hudson asked.

'It's cholera.'

Hudson felt his heart drop. He knew that cholera was an infectious disease that had a high death rate, and was easily spread.

'Hudson, will you look after the hospital, while I look after my dear Sarah.'

'Of course! Of course, I will.'

He ran to the hospital, praying as he went. For the rest of that evening Hudson Taylor attended to the patients in the little hospital.

Meanwhile Dr Parker nursed his wife devotedly through the night and into the next day. But, despite her husband's tender care, Mrs Parker died. William Parker was distraught. He was now left to care for their five children, the youngest not yet a year old.

Parker inevitably was now unable to continue running the hospital, and even began to plan to return to Scotland. So, Hudson Taylor took over the responsibility of the hospital, adding to his already heavy workload.

Limited finance was also a problem for the medical work, as most of the treatment was offered free of charge. Hudson advised the hospital staff that he could not guarantee them any wages, and some of them reluctantly left. His report of the problem to the congregation at Bridge Street had two immediate results. They prayed for more money for the work and some in the congregation began to help in the hospital. One of these new assistants was Wang Lea-djun. He also began to teach scholars in the associated school to read the Scriptures.

Hudson's extra activities in the hospital meant he had to cut back his work in the Bridge Street Church, so a heavier load also fell upon John Jones. Despite this the Bridge Street Mission began to grow.

While the ministry at Bridge Street might seem insignificant, the rationale and work of this mission was the seed out of which the China Inland Mission would sprout and grow. And the CIM became a great work.

CHAPTER 12

ENGLAND AND THE
CHINA INLAND MISSION

'We are wearing down and must have help' (Hudson Taylor to his father).

By 1860 Hudson Taylor was exhausted and ill. He had chest and liver problems and was worn out from excessive labour. He returned to England with his family for a while, though his intentions were not only to regain his health. He also planned to use his time in England to stir up interest in mission to China and recruit at least five new missionaries. How long would they stay in England? *Two years, maybe a bit longer*, they thought.

Hudson also decided to take Wang Lea-djun with them. It was a big step and a big responsibility for Wang, whom Hudson believed could help them produce translations of the Scriptures in a Romanised script, rather than the traditional pictorial script, as well as teaching Chinese to missionary candidates.

It was not easy for Hudson to leave China. He later wrote, 'To me it seemed a great calamity that failure of health compelled my relinquishing work for God in China, just when it was more fruitful than ever before; and to leave the little band of Christians in Ningpo, needing much care and teaching, was a great sorrow.'

Yet on 19 July, Hudson, Maria, Grace and Wang sailed from China aboard the new tea clipper *Jubilee*. The voyage was rough and each of them suffered from sea-sickness, Maria badly so. In addition, the captain was bad-tempered and violent, which made the trip even more unpleasant. They arrived at Gravesend on the south-east coast of England on 20 November and settled in Bayswater in Central London.

Two of the first people they met were Amelia, Hudson's sister, and the man who had become her husband a year earlier, Hudson's old friend Benjamin Broomhall. One of the first pieces of news that they heard was that the CES had just been dissolved, a sad but probably inevitable event.

At first Hudson's health improved, but in December he had a relapse. He went to see Dr Andrew Clarke, one of his old teachers at the London Hospital. Dr Clarke examined him thoroughly. But his diagnosis was as gloomy as his expression.

'My dear Taylor, there is no way you can go back to China. At least not for several years! Your digestion, liver, even your nervous system, are all seriously impaired. To go back soon would be a death sentence.'

Hudson heard the news and felt as gloomy as Dr Clarke looked. 'But I must go back,' he protested. 'There's so much to be done. Millions are dying without Christ.' He hesitated for a moment. 'What must I do to get better?'

Clarke rubbed his chin as he paused for thought. 'Well, I repeat that you must not go back soon. And I would recommend that you don't go at all.' He shrugged, knowing that Hudson's mind was made up to return. 'But if you must return, don't rush it. Take your time, rest and get back on an English diet.'

Hudson nodded. 'Thank you, Dr Clarke. I will.'

The visit to the doctor caused Hudson to rethink. He was still determined to return to China, but he began to see advantages in staying in England for longer than the originally proposed two years. He decided to contact various mission agencies, to encourage them in their missionary efforts and to stress the needs of China, and especially the interior.

He had also come to realise that medicine was a means of reaching the Chinese. He decided to further his medical studies to both help the people and make his ministry more effective. In May of 1861 he began additional studies at the London Hospital. He qualified as a Member of the Royal College of Surgeons (MRCS) little more than 14 months later.

Four more children were born to Hudson and Maria while they were in England. Herbert Hudson was born on 3 April 1861, Frederick Howard (known as Freddie or Howard) on 25 November 1862, and Samuel Dyer on 24 June 1864.

Maria fell pregnant again in the spring of 1865. It proved to be a difficult pregnancy. By the end of November, she was in such a poor state that Hudson 'felt very serious alarm about her.' On December 5, an obstetrician advised that the birth should be induced. Jane Dyer Taylor was born two days later. But little Jane died within an hour. This left Maria's health in a 'very precarious state,' and, inevitably, both she and Hudson suffered emotionally.

However, their extended period in England gave Hudson more time for thought about how the gospel could be taken to the millions of Chinese, and the main idea that kept coming to him was to move inland. But to do that effectively he needed many more helpers, many more than the five originally planned. So, he turned first to the Bible, and the Bible moved him to pray for more 'labourers.' In addition, Hudson and Maria gathered around them a small group to pray for this work.

Amongst this group was William Berger, a wealthy business man, who attended the Brook Street Chapel in Tottenham. Berger was about 15 years older than Hudson, outwardly stern, but kind, and a great man of prayer. Hudson Taylor formed a close friendship with him.

The recruiting progressed slowly. Hudson was involved in sending a man to China in January 1862, a woman two years later and three more missionaries in 1865, thus the planned five were sent. Wang Lea-djun also returned to China towards the end of this period, after assisting with the Romanised script edition of the New Testament in Chinese.

Alongside the slow-moving recruiting process, Hudson continued his medical studies and continued to plan for his return to China. He studied the map of China, with its vast interior, and wondered how it could all be reached. He began to realise the need for an organisation that focused its main attention upon inland China, but his mind was full of doubts as to how this could be established.

On Sunday 25 June 1865, a date which was to become indelibly written in his memory, he attended a church service in Brighton on England's south-eastern coast. Hudson seems to have left the service early and wandered out on a nearby beach in 'great spiritual agony'. He later recorded that he was 'unable to bear the sight of a congregation of a thousand or more Christian people rejoicing in their own security, while millions were perishing'. It was, he continued, 'There the Lord conquered my unbelief, and I surrendered myself for this service'. The thinking and planning of months crystallised almost in a moment. He prayed to God for 24 more missionaries, two for each of the eleven inland Chinese provinces and two for Mongolia. And he would lead them.

To inspire interest in this cause, Hudson wrote a booklet called *China's Spiritual Need and Claims*, which was funded by William Berger, and he also began to speak at Missionary Conferences around the country to present the needs of China. One by one people came forward to enlist for service in China. By this time Hudson and Maria had moved to Coborn Street in East London, near the London Hospital, and they invited the candidates to move into their home for training. When their home could hold no more, they rented the house next door to cope with the overflow.

Hudson had already begun to meet regularly with William Berger to plan the venture. It was decided that Berger would stay in England to supervise the needs of the Mission from there, while Hudson and his family would return to China with the team they were putting together.

'For my immediate plans I think we'll need another 15 or 16 missionaries,' said Hudson.

'That many?' responded Berger.

'Yes, I think so. We already have ten, and we should be able to raise another five or six in the new year. God is answering our prayers.'

'Indeed! But how are we going to pay for their support? I mean fares to China, clothes and other supplies. Money for rent! That's not going to be easy.'

'God will supply it.'

Berger was calculating. 'We'll need at least £1,500, and probably £2,000, and we don't have anything like that much. We've only a little over £270.'

'God will supply it.'

'Are you still against asking people for money?'

'Oh, yes!' Hudson said firmly. 'We will only ask our Heavenly Father. Look what Mr Müller has done in Bristol. He never asks anyone for a penny. And God feeds hundreds of orphans.'

'Yes, I know.'

'However, I am writing some articles about the needs of China and the people who are offering for the work. I'm thinking of putting those in a pamphlet. We could send it out to people we know are interested in the work. If it leads them to donate, then that's well and good, but I won't be asking.'

'That sounds good. Do you mean to make that a regular thing?'

'Well, I was thinking of doing it occasionally. As information comes to hand! An occasional paper, I suppose you'd call it.'

'Right! If you give me the articles, I'll see the paper is printed and distributed.'

'Good! But prayer is the important thing. I'm convinced of it.'

'And when do we send the first group to China?'

Hudson thought for a moment. 'May next year would be good.'

By the time the first *Occasional Paper* of the newly formed China Inland Mission was printed in March 1866, their funds had increased to over £2,000. And that figure was doubled in the following two months. God had indeed supplied the Mission's needs, just as Hudson had said He would.

On February 2, an important meeting had been held at the Taylors' home in Coborn Street, which effectively launched the China Inland Mission. Present were Hudson Taylor, William Berger, and prospective missionaries, James Williamson, William Rudland, Lewis Nicol and George Duncan. It would be fair to say that Hudson Taylor was the dominant voice in that meeting and in determining CIM policy generally. He, under God, was to direct 'the affairs of the Mission.' This was not unreasonable, as Hudson was the only one of this group with first-hand experience of China and its problems.

The primary aim of the Mission was to take the gospel of Jesus Christ to the Chinese, particularly those who lived inland away from existing missionary influence. However, their base would initially be in Ningpo on the coast. The meeting decided that all the Mission's 'helpers must be satisfied that God had called them to labour in China for the good of the Chinese.' They also 'must look to God for their support, and trust Him to provide it, and not lean on' Hudson Taylor or any other human being or agency. In other words, they should trust Him 'who has said, "Seek ye first the kingdom of God and his righteousness, and all these things shall be added unto you."'

However, they were expected to work under Hudson Taylor's 'guidance and direction.' Hudson would decide the nature of the work each would conduct and where they would conduct it, be it running a school or engaging in 'pioneering work.' For his part, he would help them financially as funds became available, and, where possible, assist them in any other necessary way. It was expected that all members of the Mission would wear Chinese clothing in China.

The prospective missionaries came from different denominations, so had varied views on such issues as the mode and timing of baptism, but they were all evangelicals. In fact, the missionaries Taylor was assembling around him included Methodists, Presbyterians, Baptists, Congregationalists, Anglicans and members of the Plymouth Brethren. The meeting decided that each would be allowed to follow their conscience on non-essential matters.

Hudson Taylor knew that while European missionaries were needed to take the Gospel of Christ to the Chinese, he realised that they could not win China for Christ. Hudson believed that a truly indigenous church was essential for that to happen. But that would take time.

A shipping agent advised Hudson Taylor that he and his companions could have the entire passenger accommodation aboard the tea clipper *Lammermuir*. Hudson went to see the ship, liked what he saw and paid the necessary fares.

Hudson Taylor knew that prayer was essential for successful missionary endeavour, and as always he set the example. He prayed earnestly and encouraged others to do the same. After hearing Hudson Taylor pray at a meeting at this time, one man said, 'I was deeply impressed with the simplicity and fervour of his prayer, and felt that he was speaking to a familiar Friend in whom he had perfect confidence.'

CHAPTER 13

BACK TO CHINA

In China 'a million a month are dying without God' (Hudson Taylor).

On 26 May 1866, the *Lammermuir* set sail for China with 22 missionaries on board, including the Taylors' four children. The other members of this pioneering party were the recently married Lewis and Eliza Nicol, George Duncan, Josiah Jackson, William Rudland, John Sell, James Williamson, Susan Barnes, Mary Bausum, Emily Blatchley (later governess to the Taylor children), Mary Bell, Mary Bowyer, Louise Desgraz, Jane (Jennie) Faulding, Jane McLean and Elizabeth Rose. That was seven men, ten women and five children. (Mary Bausum, a daughter of missionaries and a relative of the Taylors, was only 15 years of age, so still a child.) Most of the party were from the south of England and from Scotland. Louise Desgraz was Swiss. It was the largest group of missionaries sent to China at one time by any agency up until that time. Each of them knew that the life expectancy of a missionary in China was on average seven years.

A short while before they left England the CIM sent out a 'Special Daily Prayer' leaflet containing all their names to supporters, and urging them 'Brethren pray for us.' And, well before they arrived in China, they needed that prayer.

The *Lammermuir* was a square-rigged sailing vessel and had been built only two years previously. It was about 61 metres long and 11 across the beam. Its Master, Captain M. Bell, had been a Christian for two years. He proved to be most supportive of the party, but the brutal and bad-tempered First Mate, John Brunton, was not. The crew of over 30 men and boys came from Britain, Sweden, Germany, the South Sea Islands and the Caribbean, a mission field in itself.

As the *Lammermuir* pulled out from the dock the missionaries sang a hymn. Brunton was furious. 'I want nowt of this religious nonsense', he muttered aggressively. 'Don't tell me we're gunna get this all the way to China.'

Throughout the early part of the voyage he continued to show a strong dislike of the missionaries and repeatedly made himself objectionable. He also often unleashed his fury with his fists on some of the younger members of the crew.

The trip was neither fast nor easy. The Suez Canal, which would give a much quicker journey to Asia, was well on its way to being completed but would not be open for another three years. It was still necessary to go around the southern-most tip of Africa to reach China.

The first part of the voyage was largely trouble free. Even the waters in the Bay of Biscay were reasonably calm. Meals were ample and were eaten leisurely. The missionary party held services regularly, and these were attended by some of the crew. They read Christian books and studied Chinese. But Hudson felt a little concerned that his companions might become too content with the easy life on board. He knew it would be much tougher in China and he wanted to prepare them for that.

In the end matters were taken out of his hands. As they sailed quietly out into the Atlantic, a rogue wave suddenly smashed into the port side of the *Lammermuir*. The ship rocked violently. Hudson was nearly thrown off his feet, but managed to hold on to a rail. Simultaneously, he heard screams and shouts from the cabins on the port side and rushed around via the stern to find out if everybody was okay. As he approached the cabins he saw water pouring out from under the doors.

'Oh, no!' a man cried out. 'May the Lord preserve us!'

'Help! Help!' shouted a female voice from another cabin.

One by one cabin doors burst open and more water gushed out on to the deck. Then nine bedraggled adults and one little boy, Herbert Taylor, emerged from their cabins. (Herbert was sharing a cabin with John Sell.) It was a hot day and the portholes of each cabin had been opened and a torrent of water had rushed through each, soaking almost everything, including the occupants. The next couple of days were spent trying to dry clothes and bedding and encouraging those who had had their possessions soiled by the sea water.

At first Hudson was saddened by the predicament. But then he thought, *They'll meet worse than that in China. Perhaps it's good preparation.*

As it happened they were to meet worse than that before they reached China. They continued, for the most part, in good conditions, and, at the end of July, rounded the Cape of Good Hope. But tensions began to arise amongst the group, not least about the subject of baptism. So many people with strong beliefs together in such a small space did not always lead to smooth relationships. Petty jealousies also emerged. Hudson did his best to settle the differences.

However, the missionaries still found time to study the Bible with some of the crew, and a few of the sailors came to trust in Christ, including William Tosh, the Second Mate. Even Mr Brunton, the aggressive First Mate, began to show some interest. In fact, Brunton was now prepared to talk 'religion', particularly with Susan Barnes and Hudson Taylor. However, he had a Roman Catholic background so he disagreed on just about everything, often in an argumentative and unpleasant manner.

One day Hudson asked Brunton, 'Will you read the Bible with me?'

'The Bible? You trying to convert me like you've done with the others?'

Hudson, who was not in the best of health, thought it best to ignore the questions. 'Well, will you?'

Brunton hesitated and breathed a deep sigh. 'Well, maybe! Well, yes, I will. But don't 'spect me to believe it. My priest warned me about people like you.'

A little later that day, Hudson Taylor met with Brunton and read through the first three chapters of the Letter to the Romans. At first the reading was interrupted by the First Mate's disagreeable commentary. But as it proceeded, Brunton gradually became silent.

'You can see, can't you, Mr Brunton, we are all sinners?'

Brunton knew that he certainly was, but he was reluctant to admit it. He just grunted.

'And that Christ died for us?'

Brunton grunted again.

Taylor realised that that was about as far as they were going to get that day, so he left it there.

The next day they met again and this time Hudson read through Romans chapters four and five. Brunton listened in silence.

When he had finished reading, Hudson fired questions at the now subdued man. 'Do you see that this passage is about access to God and having peace with God? Don't you want peace with God?'

Brunton remained silent.

'Jesus Christ died for us. And rose again! We all need to be put right with God and that can only happen if we have faith in Christ. The Scripture says, "Therefore being justified by faith, we have peace with God through our Lord Jesus Christ." Peace with God! Don't you want that?'

Brunton was clearly struggling. He said nothing for a minute or two, but his face betrayed his agony. Hudson Taylor was praying silently for him.

Then Brunton spoke. 'But not for me! Not for me!'

'Yes, for you. The Scripture says, "But God commendeth his love toward us, in that, while we were yet sinners, Christ died for us."'

'But not for me!'

Brunton's look told Hudson that that was enough for the day, so he left it there and with God.

Later that day the winds blew stronger and the clipper pitched and tossed in the waves. Hudson heard Brunton barking out orders to the crew, with a string of swear words. The wild weather battered the ship for several days, preventing Hudson from having any further conversations with the First Mate.

But the missionaries met to pray for Brunton, and, when conditions allowed, William Tosh met with some other members of the crew to pray for him.

When the weather eased a little, Hudson met with Brunton again. This time they read together Exodus 12, the story of the Passover. They talked for about two hours. Brunton mainly listened, though he made brief comments and asked an occasional question. But his face remained blank and hard.

'You see that when the blood of a lamb was applied to the doorposts, the angel of death passed by that house,' said Hudson. 'For "When I see the blood," God said, "I will pass over you." Those occupants of the houses marked with blood lived. The blood, as it were, protected them from judgment. It's like that with the blood of Jesus Christ. He is the Lamb of God. We're all sinful, but when we believe in Him His blood cleanses us from all our sin. The punishment we deserve for our wickedness is removed.'

Brunton became silent. He was clearly thinking.

'You remember what we saw in Romans the other day,' continued Hudson. "God hath set forth" Jesus "to be a propitiation through faith in his blood. For the remission of sins!" That means Jesus has borne our punishment. God's anger has been poured out on Him. If we repent and believe in Him, the judgement for our sins has been removed.'

Brunton was listening intently. Suddenly, his face changed. The Spirit had broken through.

'I see! I see!' He paused as God's Spirit moved within him. 'How blind I've been. I believe! I believe!' His voice rose in intensity with each brief sentence. Then he burst forth in praise to God.

Hudson Taylor listened with joy to the outpouring of a newly grace-touched heart. Then he too burst forth in praise.

The next day Hudson Taylor wrote, 'Mr Brunton feels his burden quite gone, and all the party are overjoyed.' So, indeed, were the crew. No more did the First Mate treat them badly.

The journey continued through the Indian Ocean and the seas again became rough. One Sunday in August a sailor named McDougall was out on the jib boom at the bow of the ship. Suddenly, the vessel rolled and McDougall lost his grip. As he fell he managed to grab hold of one of the ropes attached to the boom. The wind and the waves continued to pound the ship and his grip once more slipped, so he fell again. But this time he managed to grab hold of one of the stays beneath the boom. He was by this time semi-conscious, having banged his head in the fall. But somehow he held on, seemingly by instinct.

Henry Elliott, another sailor, had seen the fall. 'Man overboard!' he cried. 'Man overboard!' However, not many heard him, as the wind howled and the waves continued to smash into the *Lammermuir*. Elliott assessed the situation quickly. *If someone doesn't get to him soon, he's a gonner*, he thought. So, Elliott climbed over the ship rail and began to inch his way along the stay. Several times he nearly lost his grip in the fierce winds. But he reached McDougall and held him in position.

By this time Second Mate Tosh and a couple of other sailors had seen the emergency and rushed to the bow of the ship. Tosh grabbed a secured rope, and he too edged his way out on the stay to where Elliott was desperately holding on to McDougall. As Elliott held the poor man in position, Tosh tied the rope around the fallen sailor. Elliott then loosened McDougall's grip on the stay, and the sailors on board ship pulled him aboard. After that Tosh and Elliott successfully made the precarious return journey to the safety of the ship.

The storm had damaged the *Lammermuir*, but, when it eased, some in the missionary party, which included two carpenters and two blacksmiths, helped the sailors with the repairs.

But the dangers were not over. On September 10, a fierce cyclone hit them while they were traversing the South China Sea. For more than four days it raged, 'with wild sea and the rain descending as if the clouds were coming down bodily.' Then calm came and they sailed into the Pacific.

After a week of serenity another cyclone hit them. This one was even worse than its predecessor. According to Hudson Taylor, it was 'a stiffer gale than any we had yet had.' The jib boom gave way, some of the sails were torn to shreds, the bulwarks on the starboard side were washed away, giving entry to the sea, and most of the casks holding their fresh water were washed overboard. If all that was not bad enough, Captain Bell was ill. The terrible weather had stretched him to the limits of endurance. His face was partly paralysed and in that condition he found it difficult to cope with such a severe emergency.

Hudson Taylor later remembered 'The appearance of things was now truly terrific. The ship was rolling fearfully, the masts and yards hanging down were tearing our only sail and battering like a ram against the main yard. The deck from forecastle to poop was one scarcely broken sea. The roar of the water, the clanging of chains, the beating of the dangling masts and yards, the sharp smack of the torn sails made it almost impossible to hear any orders that might be given.'

Jennie Faulding later recorded 'It seemed impossible that we should weather the storm. I am glad to say we were all kept calm and ready for life or death.' The sailors struggled desperately to keep the ship afloat and they all prayed that they would be spared.

For a while it even appeared that the China Inland Mission would sink on its first voyage: Sink with its founder and first missionaries, never to emerge again. But God had a purpose for them all and for the Mission they were part of.

This storm, at its worst, only lasted for three days, but they were three frightening days. As it eased, sailors and missionaries, including the women, manned the pumps and did what repairs they could. The ship had become, in Hudson Taylor's words, 'broken and dismantled', but it managed to limp safely into Shanghai harbour on 30 September 1866.

Hudson Taylor believed that if the CIM party had not been on board the *Lammermuir* it may not have arrived safely in Shanghai. He said, 'the moral influence of the *passengers* (ladies not excepted) working to save the ship was I believe the means of inducing the men to do their duty instead of giving way to despair.'

Maria Taylor had become pregnant again just before they had left England and she had a terrible time on this voyage. Whether it was morning sickness or sea sickness mattered little, for she suffered it for most of the journey, which weakened her considerably. Hudson, too, had been ill in the latter part of the journey.

First Mate Brunton was baptised in Shanghai and remained true to the faith. When he returned to England he visited William and Mary Berger to report on the missionary party's venture. On later visits to China he kept in touch with some members of the China Inland Mission. The *Lammermuir* was lost at sea in the middle of 1876, while travelling from Calcutta (Kolkata) to Demerara (part of Guyana). It is not known whether Brunton was still with that clipper, and by that time Captain Bell, who had been seriously ill since returning to England, had been replaced by a Captain Smart.

CHAPTER 14

A WIDER MINISTRY

'God grant that having been brought to the gates of eternity and then spared for a while our lives may be totally devoted to Him, and the work before us' (Jennie Faulding).

Captain Bell gave permission for the CIM missionaries to stay aboard the *Lammermuir* while they sorted, cleaned and dried their water-damaged possessions. This was not a problem to Bell as the *Lammermuir* was not going anywhere until major repairs had been made, which would take some weeks.

The Christian community in Shanghai, or at least most of it, were expecting the new arrivals, and various individuals gave them a warm welcome and practical assistance. On the first evening after their arrival William Gamble of the American Presbyterian Mission Press visited them.

He held out his hand and warmly shook Hudson Taylor's. 'Welcome, Hudson. It is wonderful to see you again. God be praised that you've arrived safely. It was a rough voyage, I understand.'

Hudson smiled grimly. 'Yes, it was. Very rough! But the Lord said that he would "safely keep" us. And He did. Let me introduce you to the other missionaries of the China Inland Mission.' So, Hudson made the introductions. Then Gamble gave Hudson an update on what had been going on in China, particularly in Shanghai and Ningpo, while the Taylors had been in Britain.

'And do you have anywhere to stay, Hudson?' Gamble asked.

'Yes, Captain Bell has very kindly agreed to allow us to stay on board the *Lammermuir* while repairs are going on. That will give us time to find somewhere. Though, to be frank, I feel we might be in the way.'

'I've been thinking. I've a large warehouse, mainly unused. It has equipment and stocks of books and things, but there's plenty of room. You could use that for a base if you wish. There's even living accommodation attached to it.'

Hudson thought for a moment. 'Yes, that's most kind.'

So, Hudson went and inspected the property and accepted Gamble's offer. Then bit by bit the CIM missionaries took their possessions and equipment into the warehouse and eventually moved in. While still in the process of moving into the warehouse, Hudson Taylor took his new helpers around Shanghai to give them firsthand experience of the Chinese way of life and to hear Chinese spoken.

Shanghai by this time was a much more peaceful city than when Hudson had first arrived more than ten years before. The Taiping rebellion that was going on at that time had been crushed. However, in the north-west of China a new rebellion had begun that could influence how and where Hudson would send his people.

Hudson was initially thinking of sending two missionaries to the capital cities in each of the Chinese provinces, and, with those who had earlier arrived in China, he had just about enough to do that. Then as each team established a successful work in their city they would spread the good news to other towns in their province with the help of Chinese converts and additional missionaries. It was a grand nation-wide plan, which was later amended for practical reasons. However, Hudson never had less than the whole country in mind.

Amongst the missionaries Hudson had earlier sent out to China from Britain were James Meadows and John Stevenson. At about the time that the *Lammermuir* party left England these two men, with the Chinese basket weaver Feng Nenggui, went on a brief visit to Shaohsing, 160 kilometres inland from Ningpo. A few months later a Chinese Christian moved to Shaohsing, a town with a population of 250,000, to follow up their ministry and to establish a church. John and Annie Stevenson moved to Shaohsing to support him a few weeks later. Hudson Taylor's plan to reach the interior of China had begun to take shape even before he had returned to China.

Shanghai already had a significant missionary community, and Ningpo, home of the Bridge Street Church, also had a small but vibrant Christian ministry. So, Hudson Taylor decided to settle in neither. He chose as his base Hangchow in Chekiang province, which was situated between those two cities and a little to the west. It was not one of the treaty ports.

There was a delay of three weeks before they were able to get the required documents to move inland. This gave those new to China opportunity to get used to wearing Chinese clothing and eating Chinese food. It also gave them more time to learn the language.

Then late in October the entire party with Chinese helpers, including Mr Tsiu, an able evangelist, began the journey in four junks along the Huangpu River to Hangchow. William Gamble came to see them off.

As he boarded the boat, Hudson Taylor shook hands with him. 'And how much rent do we owe you for our using your property', Hudson asked.

Gamble thought for a moment. 'Let it stand at one hundred dollars.'

'And that's it?'

'Yes, that'll be fine.'

Hudson handed over the money in a small purse.

'Thank you!'

When Gamble prepared to leave, he shook hands with Hudson and his companions and smiled at Hudson. As he disembarked, Gamble deliberately placed the purse still full of money on the deck of the junk. Hudson moved forward to pick it up to return it to him, but Gamble was already ashore and heading home.

A little later they set off. In the early part of the journey they passed the *Lammermuir*, which was still undergoing repairs. The four junks pulled alongside the clipper and the missionaries offered their greetings and farewells. The sailors responded warmly.

Susan Barnes later remembered 'It was most solemn to see strong, rough men bowed down and weeping bitterly. Then just as we moved off they began the verse "Pilgrims, may we travel with you?" They then climbed the ropes and shouted "Hurrah!" for as long as we could hear them.'

***

Hangchow was a major city that had suffered badly during the Taiping rebellion, but was now being rebuilt. However, this rebuilding still had a long way to go. They arrived there on 21 November. Hudson Taylor and Mr Tsiu had just begun the difficult search for accommodation when they received a message from Carl Kreyer, an American Baptist missionary. He lived in Hangchow with his wife, but they were, at that time, visiting Ningpo. The message said that the CIM party could use his rented home while he was out of town. This, at least, gave them a roof over their heads while they looked for somewhere else.

Taylor and Tsiu returned to the boats on the canal and told their companions the good news. 'But there is one problem,' said Hudson.

'Which is?' said one.

Hudson smiled. 'Well, if we all arrive at the house in one go in daylight we might cause a riot. The people might think it's an invasion.'

Some of the missionaries let out an audible sigh of relief. A few laughed.

'Let's all get ready to leave the boats. When it gets dark we will walk in small groups to Mr Kreyer's house. Mr Tsiu will give you directions.'

Hudson organised them into two main groups. When darkness fell the first party gathered its possessions together and began to walk to Kreyer's house, led by Tsiu. When they drew close they split into smaller groups and finished the journey. When the remaining missionaries decided that they had given the others enough time they did the same thing, led by Hudson Taylor. They all arrived without alarm.

However, they could not stay there forever. First it was too small; secondly, Mr and Mrs Kreyer would need it back. Even though Hudson's intention was to send the missionaries to different places, he still needed a central place with living space, and room for preaching, a printing press and a dispensary. So, the search for larger premises began.

At this point the earlier rebellion came to their aid. On the east of the city, in New Lane, they discovered a derelict, two-story building with around 30 rooms. The house itself was anything but 'new' and it needed a lot of work, but they had the workforce to do it. Amongst the missionary band were two blacksmiths, one of whom also had skills with machines, and two carpenters, plus other willing workers.

Hudson and Tsiu began negotiations with the owner, but he asked a ridiculously high rent and was unwilling to move far from that figure. So, they left him. The next day was Sunday, which they made a day of prayer. On Monday they began to look for another building. The owner of the New Lane premises heard that they were doing so, and realising he might lose a reliable tenant, he caught up with them and named a lower price for his property. Hudson still thought this price too high and began bargaining. Finally, they settled on a price, and the CIM missionaries took charge of 1 New Lane and began renovations.

There were already a few Chinese living in the building, and Taylor and his companions had no objection to them remaining there. They presented an on-the-spot mission field.

Even while the renovations were being carried out, Hudson was thinking ahead. At about this time James Meadows and George Crombie, two of the missionaries Hudson had sent out earlier from England, returned from an exploratory trip and visited the new CIM headquarters. They suggested that the town of Xiaoshan, a little south of Hangchow on the other side of the Tsientang River, would be a strategic place to base two of his troops. Hudson went with them to check it out and agreed, and he began to plan who to send.

Early in December Maria Taylor, about seven months pregnant, made a return visit to Ningpo, along with Meadows and Crombie. The primary aim of this visit was to enlist some Chinese Christians to come and work in Hangchow. The Taylors always recognised that if China was to be evangelised, then Chinese Christians must play the major part. Maria returned in the middle of the month with several men and two women. On another visit to Ningpo a little later Maria took Jane McLean with her. This was to increase McLean's experience of China.

These ventures by Maria Taylor were very brave. Her health had been poor since the time she had been pregnant with Jane, the child who had died soon after birth in December 1865. The traumatic sea journey to China while she was again pregnant was a terrible time for her, and had continuing after effects. On 3 February 1867 Maria gave birth to a daughter, who they named Maria Hudson.

Soon after their arrival Jennie Faulding began to minister to the other residents in the New Lane building. She became particularly close to a woman named Alosoa. They often spoke to each other. Jennie found that what she said was usually understood by her new-found friend, though it was not always easy for Jennie to understand her. Alosoa became fascinated by what Jennie told her about Christ and began to pray to Him.

The Chinese of the New Lane area inevitably became curious about this large number of foreigners in their midst and began to visit Mission HQ and ask questions. The CIM people were now all dressed in Chinese clothing, but this did not hide the fact that they were foreigners. However, that Chinese clothing seems to have made them more approachable.

Hudson did not miss the opportunity. He did his best to answer their questions and invited them to the regular Sunday services, to which some of them came. Alosoa also brought other Chinese along. On the last Sunday in 1866 they held two public services, each with over 50 people present. After the meetings some of the Chinese stayed behind to ask questions.

Hudson had by this time changed his strategy for evangelising China. Rather than scattering his forces throughout China, he decided to establish the work province by province. His first focus was on the province of Chekiang, which had eleven prefectures. These included Ningpo and Hangchow, which already had missionaries in residence. They had been unable to get into one of the others, Kiahsing, so Hudson's plan now was to establish missions in the other eight prefectures in that province. If they could follow that plan of reaching one province at a time, they would have a chance of eventually conquering the whole of China.

One especially attractive target was Wenchow, over 300 kilometres to the south of Hangchow. Hudson Taylor sent along George Stott, a one-legged Scot. Stott was a fairly experienced missionary, having been in China since late 1865. Another important town was Taichow, about 230 kilometres to the south-east. Hudson sent James Meadows with Josiah Jackson and a Chinese Christian to start the work there. Later William Rudland, by this time married to Mary Bell, replaced them when they moved on. Hudson also despatched Lewis and Eliza Nicol and James Williamson to Xiaoshan, just a little over 15 kilometres away. They all had the necessary permits to live in these places. In this way, region by region was to be evangelised.

Wang Lae-djun, the man who had gone to Britain with the Taylors, had served with a Methodist mission in Ningpo since his return to China. Early in 1867 Hudson Taylor began to think that Wang would be a good man to lead the work in Hangchow. Later that year when Wang was able to leave Ningpo, he and his wife travelled to Hangchow to join the CIM party. With Wang's arrival, Hudson was relieved of some of his responsibilities, giving him greater opportunity to supervise the expansion of the Mission.

CHAPTER 15

MANY KINDS OF TROUBLE

'Our Jesus hath done all things well' (Hymn 233, *Psalms, Hymns and Spiritual Songs*, Boston: 1802).

Hudson Taylor always expected to have difficulties in taking the Gospel to the Chinese. He knew that there would be opposition from the national people and that sometimes he would experience danger. What he did not expect was opposition from those in his own and other missions, at least not in any significant form. Hudson's practice was to allow each missionary to develop their ministry in their own way, depending on their local circumstances, providing it did not conflict with neighbouring missions and overall CIM policy. However, even before they had reached Hangchow there had been one or two mild arguments amongst some of the women in the missionary party, and some more agitated incidents amongst two of the men. The reality of many people from such different backgrounds living so close together was that relationships were sometimes strained.

George Moule was a CMS missionary in Ningpo and Hangchow, with strong Anglican convictions. His father had shown friendship towards Hudson Taylor during the latter's return to England. George Moule's missionary methods were different from Hudson Taylor's. In China Moule continued to live and dress as a European. He also held strongly to Anglican doctrine and methods, particularly about baptism. That is, he regarded infant baptism as a perfectly legitimate method of baptism. In the CIM Hudson Taylor and his associates believed that each CIM missionary should follow his or her own conscience on such matters as the mode and timing of baptism.

Some of this first CIM party were Anglicans or at least had Anglican connections back in England. It appears that soon after the party's arrival in China, two of these were baptised or (depending on one's beliefs) re-baptised, as in Baptist circles. This aroused Moule's resentment, though at first he said nothing.

At that time Lewis Nicol of the *Lammermuir* party was also becoming uneasy about Hudson Taylor, with grievances more imaginary than real. Nicol was an imposing man, a powerfully-built blacksmith, with a strong personality. He objected to the idea of missionaries wearing Chinese dress. But CIM had a clear rule that its missionaries should wear Chinese clothing. That was a point on which Taylor would not give way. This placed Nicol in direct disagreement with Taylor, the undisputed leader of CIM. So here were two powerful personalities in the same movement with opposing views.

Lewis Nicol became friendly with George Moule. Nicol was a Presbyterian, so he agreed with Moule on infant baptism. He also agreed with him on the issue of what clothing missionaries should wear. This friendship was bound to sow discontent, both in CIM and the wider missionary community. Moule's support strengthened Nicol's resolve.

After Nicol's move to Xiaoshan he began to wear European clothes again. He made a brief return to Hangchow, still dressed in European clothing. Hudson Taylor was not pleased, but decided to say nothing at the time.

It had previously been planned that Mr Tsiu would help in establishing the Mission in Xiaoshan, so when Nicol returned there Tsiu went with him. On the following Sunday they and James Williamson held morning and evening services, which attracted good numbers. The next day they ventured out into the market place. Tsiu preached the Gospel and Nicol and Williamson stood beside him in support. Nicol was still wearing European clothing, Williamson Chinese.

A crowd quickly gathered and its response was explosive. The people screamed their opposition.

'Foreign devils! Foreign devils! Death to the foreign devils!' It seemed to make no difference that Tsiu was as Chinese as they were, and even Williamson was dressed like them.

The mob moved in menacingly on the Christians. Their manner was especially threatening towards Nicol, whom they seem to have taken a strong dislike to. The three missionaries backed away and managed to escape to their home. The crowd followed for a while still shouting and screaming, but soon lost interest.

That evening there was a disturbance outside their house. It was a crowd carrying lanterns, and amidst it was the local mandarin in a sedan chair. Then there was a loud and persistent knock at the door. Nicol opened it, and two officers rushed in, pushing him out of the way. Then the mandarin entered, followed by more of his retainers.

The mandarin was at first polite, but soon began to bark questions and orders to Nicol and Williamson and to his own people. He gave little more than a glance at Tsiu. His manner was aggressive and unpleasant.

When he finished his interrogation of the two missionaries he turned his attention to Tsiu. He signalled to two of his men and they forced Tsiu down on the floor. Two others then began to beat the poor man's legs repeatedly with bamboos. Tsiu screamed in agony. The blood flowed. When that fearful deed was done, one man drew out a leather strap and proceeded to use it to beat Tsiu about the face.

When the Mandarin and his entourage departed the Nicols and Williamson nursed Tsiu, who was in a terrible state. After the beating he was only semi-conscious. They decided it was best to return to Hangchow, so the next day they made the journey and reported to Hudson Taylor.

Nicol was in a furious mood; Tsiu was barely able to speak. Taylor made sure Tsiu was cared for and then questioned Nicol about what had happened.

'We were brutally attacked,' Nicol said. 'I am going to report this to the Consul.'

'It will be better if you leave that to me. I know him well and as leader of this Mission an approach from me will carry more weight.'

Nicol scowled, but said nothing.

Hudson thought for a moment. 'You do, I assume, consider yourself a missionary of the China Inland Mission?'

Nicol looked surprised at the question, but nodded.

'Well, then, you really must take direction from me as its leader. One of our rules is that we all wear Chinese clothes. And you should do so.'

Nicol was silent for a moment, and then said, 'But European clothes give protection and respect.'

'They may have protected you, but poor Tsiu was left in an appalling state. The Chinese may accept it in the treaty ports, but they will not in these more distant parts. Tell me, will you or will you not wear Chinese clothing?'

Nicol seemed to agonise over his decision. 'If you say so!' he said quietly.

A week or two passed and still Nicol was wearing European clothes, so Hudson confronted him again.

'Mr Nicol, you are still not wearing Chinese dress. It is a rule of our Mission that we all do.'

For a while Nicol did not answer. The two men just stared at each other. Then in a voice taught with emotion, Nicol said, 'No, I won't. I will not be bound neck and heel to any man.'

Hudson Taylor paused to take that in. Then he said, 'Mr Nicol, your failure to observe this rule could prove dangerous to the Mission.

Do you realise that?'

'You exaggerate. Anyway, it might be better for me to leave the Mission and go to one of the free ports. I won't have to wear them there.'

'Yes, I think that may prove to be the best course.'

So, Lewis and Eliza Nicol left the Mission and went to work in one of the treaty ports. But that did not completely end the conflict. Two other members of CIM, John Sell and Jane McLean, who had become engaged, sympathised with the Nicols, and, while staying with the CIM, remained discontent.

***

The personal lives of Hudson and Maria Taylor during these years became increasingly difficult. In the hot summer of 1867 Maria was unwell with a fever and a bad cough and Hudson had conjunctivitis. Howard Taylor also had a fever and was suffering from convulsions, while Herbert had recently been bitten by a dog, which caused some anxiety. But worse was to come. Grace was also a little unwell. She had recently made a confession of faith and her father had baptised her, which greatly encouraged the family. On July 31 she celebrated her eighth birthday.

Soon after that the family and some of their fellow missionaries moved to a cooler spot for a few weeks to recuperate, but it did no good. Maria could barely move out of bed and Howard showed no sign of improvement. While in their retreat Hudson heard that some of his other staff were also ill, so he paid them a quick visit.

On his way back to the family he also began to get severe pains in the abdomen. When he arrived back he was met by a grim-faced Emily Blatchley. 'Gracie is worse, I'm afraid, Mr Taylor. Much worse!'

Hudson forgot his own a pain for a moment and rushed to his daughter's side. Emily followed. Grace had a severe fever and was only semi-conscious. She was mumbling something incoherently. He examined her and concluded that it was either typhus or meningitis. As he stooped over her, he prayed that God would make her well. He then stood upright again.

'Emily, apply cold compresses to Gracie. It will help bring down her temperature.'

'Yes, Mr Taylor. Immediately!'

Hudson then looked over to his wife, who was lying in a nearby bed, her face stained with tears. She smiled at him weakly. He went to her side, bent over and gently kissed her.

'Poor Gracie!' she said.

'Yes, she is most unwell, I'm afraid. Emily is going to apply cold compresses. Hopefully that will bring down her temperature. We're going to have to cut her hair to make that more effective.'

'No! No! You can't do that. Not her lovely hair!'

'But we must, my dear.'

Maria thought for a moment. 'Then *I* will cut it,' she said determinedly.

Hudson looked at his wife and realised that there was no point in arguing. He helped her from her bed and took her to where Grace was resting. Maria knelt beside the bed and cried. Hudson found a pair of scissors and gave them to her. She glared at them with a look of horror, but took them and began to cut Grace's long golden locks. When she had finished Emily began to apply the compresses.

But Hudson knew that nothing was likely to save her. He did his best to prepare Maria for the death that seemed inevitable and they wept together.

On the evening of 23 August 1867 little Grace Taylor died. She left behind two deeply saddened parents.

Early in 1868 Maria became pregnant again, and on 29 November she gave birth to Charles Edward. They now had five living children: Herbert (aged 7) Frederick Howard (6) Samuel (4), Maria (1) and Charles.

Tragedy struck repeatedly in 1870. That year Maria, with her health already in tatters, struggled through another pregnancy. The children were also unwell, and tensions between Europeans and Chinese were increasing again. So early that year Hudson and Maria decided to send their four eldest children to England, under the care of Emily Blatchley, who had been injured in a riot the previous year.

While they were still making plans for the children's departure their now five-year old son Samuel became seriously ill. Samuel had never been strong and was unable to fight the illness. The Taylors nursed him tenderly, but he died on 4 February.

Six weeks later the Taylor family, still mourning, went to Shanghai. Maria, a little better in health, refused to be left at home. On March 22 they tearfully said goodbye to their three eldest children.

'Be good, Bertie,' Hudson said to his eldest son. 'Make sure you look after Howard and Maria.'

'Yes, father. I will.' Herbert brushed a tear from his eye.

'Good boy! God bless you.'

Maria threw her arms around each of her children in turn and covered them in kisses. Then the tears flowed profusely. No one knew when, or even if, they would see each other again. Hudson and Maria found themselves remembering their most recent voyage to China, with its storms and terror. All they could do was commit their children to God in prayer. Surely, He would look after them.

Emily Blatchley, who was never to return to China, shepherded her little flock on to the ship's deck to wave farewell to their parents. As the ship pulled away, their shouts of goodbye were lost in the sounds of sea and birds.

Loss upon loss, upon loss!

But worse was to come.

As her confinement approached Maria's health declined once more. She ate little and rarely kept down what she did eat. On 7 July Maria gave birth to a son, Noel. Maria was unable to feed him and they had difficulty finding a wetnurse, so they bottle fed him. Thirteen days after he was born Noel Taylor died.

Maria's health continued the downward spiral. She was in deep emotional distress and her physical condition continued to deteriorate. But amidst all this terrible sadness came some good news. A letter arrived from Emily Blatchley: she and the children had arrived safely in England. Hudson breathed a sigh of relief. Maria cried tears of gratitude to God. They were further encouraged when a letter came from George Müller, with a cheque for their support.

One night, as Hudson nursed Maria, she became agitated and said, 'My head is so hot.'

'I will cut your hair, my dear, and apply more cold compresses.'

'Not too short! Not too short, now!'

Hudson did not know whether to laugh or cry. He knew that Maria always liked her hair long, so he cut it short but not too short. When he had finished, he said 'Shall I send a lock to each of the children?'

'Yes! Yes!' she said eagerly. 'And tell them to be kind to Miss Blatchley. And tell them to always love Jesus.' Then Maria focused her full attention upon Hudson. 'You know, my darling, I am altogether yours.' She threw her thin arms around her husband 'in her own loving way.' A few minutes later he gently broke from her weak grasp and began to apply the compresses.

On 23 July, three days after the death of Noel, it was clear that Maria was dying. Early that morning Hudson saw her pallid complexion and knew that death was close. He sat next to her and spoke to her tenderly. 'My darling, you know you are dying? You will soon be with Jesus.'

She hesitated for a moment and then said faintly, 'I am so sorry, my dear.'

'You are not sorry to go to be with Jesus, dear.'

'Oh, no! It's not that. It's not that,' she said, rising a little and looking straight at her husband. She paused briefly to catch her breath. 'There has not been a cloud between my soul and my Saviour for ten years past. I cannot be sorry to go to Him.' She paused again. 'But I am sorry to leave you alone at this time.'

But talking tired her and she sank back onto her pillow exhausted. She closed her eyes and, as Hudson prayed, she fell into a deep sleep. At 9.20 that evening she died.

This string of tragic events was enough to destroy any man, and Hudson Taylor felt each blow deeply. William Rudland said that at that time Hudson was 'very much crushed'. He certainly grieved each loss. Yet those losses did not destroy him. As he put it, 'My heart wells up with joy and gratitude for their unutterable bliss, though nigh to breaking. "Our Jesus hath done all things well."'

***

There was also wider trouble at this time. In June 1870 rumours had arisen that Catholic nuns in Tientsin in north-eastern China were kidnapping Chinese children and abusing them. On 21 June, a large and noisy crowd assembled in the town protesting against the assumed wrongdoing. The mob attacked the Catholic Cathedral, smashing its windows.

The Catholics protested to the local French Consul, who paid a hasty visit to the local magistrate. The two men argued and, in circumstances hotly debated, the Consul shot one of the magistrate's servants.

Outside, Chinese officials were trying to quieten the rioters, but when word got out about the shooting, the situation exploded. The mob attacked and killed the Consul and his assistant, dumping their bodies in the river. They then caught, raped and killed some of the nuns, and burnt the Cathedral and other western buildings.

The trouble spread south to Nanking in Kiangsu province, less than 300 kilometres from Hangchow. The local viceroy, Ma Xinyi, was a Muslim, but he did his best to keep the peace and protect Christians and other vulnerable groups. But on 22 August dissidents stabbed him to death, as the violence spread into that region.

All this greatly increased tension between the Chinese and European authorities and people, and made it more difficult for missionaries, both Catholic and Protestant, to work safely. Though the original outbreak of violence had occurred many kilometres to the north of Hangchow and Ningpo, the CIM, like other missions, was badly affected by it and continued to live under its threat.

Hudson called it 'a time of great trial.' He added 'From Peking to Canton the people were agitated. We did not know from day to day what would take place in our inland stations. But I had unspeakable rest in my soul.'

Christian mission in China was not getting easier. Yet in these troubled years more missionaries arrived from Britain to strengthen the CIM workforce. They were posted to various towns, mainly near the Yangtze River, in the provinces Chekiang and Kiangsu in the east of the country.

***

Amidst all these troubles Hudson sent a letter to Grattan Guinness, the Irish evangelist, saying, 'The difficulties and the dangers and the sicknesses and sorrows of the past year, I think I may say they have equalled if not exceeded, those of the preceding sixteen years of my missionary labour. But be this as it may, the Lord had previously taught me *practically*, as I never knew it before, our *present, real* oneness with Christ. And with the exception of the last two months, it has been the happiest and most joyous year of my life.'

CHAPTER 16

JENNIE

'A little thing is a little thing, but faithfulness in little things is a great thing' (Hudson Taylor).

Only a deep experience of God and great determination could help Hudson move on after these tragic events. And move on he did. He recognised that life was short and he, being surrounded by serious disease and conflict, might have a shorter life than most. This thought only fired him to greater effort.

He continued to plan and organise the work; he continued to write letters to supporters back in Britain. He preached, he prayed and he assisted his workers. Another responsibility was little Charles, the remaining Taylor child in China. The two-year old boy was often unwell and needed much attention. Mary Gough helped care for him. (Mary had been the wife of Hudson's good friend John Jones, who had died in 1863. She had married Frederick Gough of the CMS three years later.)

CIM held a day of fasting and prayer on December 30. At that gathering Hudson received encouraging news about the progress of CIM in various locations. There were now about 30 CIM missionaries, plus their children, and over 40 Chinese workers based in ten cities, with ministries that stretched even further afield. There were also reports of conversions and baptisms from practically every CIM station, and there were now fewer problems amongst his mission staff.

Particularly encouraging was the work in Hangchow and its

surrounding area, which Wang led. Wang followed Hudson's lead and worked for no salary, trusting God to meet his needs. The main Hangchow church in New Lane now had over 60 members, and in addition there were four outposts connected with it. The work in Wenchow and Taichow was also progressing well, with reports of more than 100 Chinese attending some meetings.

Early in 1871 Hudson Taylor became ill. Stress, sorrow, and excessive labour had laid him low. He had a bout of bronchitis and suffered ongoing pains in his back and side. At the end of March his health became so poor that he thought he was dying. He considered making Emily Blatchley the official guardian of his children, but what he did not know was that she was also unwell. Fortunately, God answered the prayers of many and his health showed some improvement.

***

Back in England William Berger, the co-founder of CIM, was also feeling the strain. He wrote to Hudson telling him, 'I bear burdens too heavy for me. I get weaker year by year.' Berger's efficient and dedicated service in England had been essential to the work in China. He recruited staff, arranged for their transport and publicised the Mission in Britain. And all this was on top of running a business. Hudson knew of no one else there willing and able to lead the work on the home front if Berger resigned or died.

There were even signs of declining interest in Britain about the CIM. It was five years since Hudson Taylor and the first CIM party had left England, and, except in some quarters, he and his colleagues had become forgotten figures. Berger wrote to Hudson urging him to make a quick visit to Britain to stimulate interest. So, Hudson decided to make another return trip to stir up support, to recruit new missionaries, to see his other children again and, hopefully, to recover his health. But was he to go alone, or should others go with him? Some of his missionary team certainly needed a break from the extremes of Chinese weather and the stresses of pioneer missionary life.

Jennie Faulding, a member of the *Lammermuir* party, had become an able and dedicated missionary. She had established a school in Hangchow, and several Chinese children had become Christians through her ministry. She had always been close to the Taylors, and had served as Hudson's assistant in Britain before going to China. Her parents were also friends of William and Mary Berger. After the death of Maria, Jennie had become like 'a sister' to Hudson Taylor.

Jennie's parents, especially her mother, were anxious that she should return home. Jennie had originally proposed to go to China for five years. Those five years were nearly up and Mrs Faulding, concerned about violence in China after the Tientsin massacre, reminded her of her original intention. After a considerable personal struggle, Jennie came to believe that it was God's will that she should return to Britain, at least for a while.

It could have been easily misunderstood if Hudson Taylor left China accompanied by Jennie Faulding, even if it was known that she would be looking after little Charlie Taylor. Victorian society would have frowned upon that. Fortunately, at that time James and Elizabeth Meadows were also planning to return. James was CIM's longest serving missionary recruit, having been in China for nine successive years. Elizabeth, as Elizabeth Rose, had been another of the *Lammermuir* party. It was agreed they should all sail together. They left China on August 5, 1871, on the French ship *Volga*, accompanied by Lanfeng, a Chinese Christian.

They arrived in Britain on September 25. Soon after their arrival Hudson's mother, Emily Blatchley and the Taylor children came south and Hudson established a home for them all and Lanfeng in Mildmay Road, Newington Green in North London.

This new arrangement was strange for all the children, but

strangest for little Charlie. He had never known anything other than China and Chinese food and ways. Here he was in unknown England, and to him it was another world. Herbert, now ten, and Howard, nearly nine, had an air of independence about them. Maria, aged four, was just glad to see her father again.

Jennie went to live with her parents in another part of the city. Inevitably Hudson Taylor and Jennie Faulding had spent time together on the voyage. They had always liked and respected each other and now felt a developing mutual love. They began to think of marriage, so Hudson approached William Faulding.

'Mr Faulding,' Hudson began, 'I wish to ask for your daughter Jane's hand in marriage.' (He used her proper name, not Jennie, for it sounded more formal.)

Faulding stood there for a few moments in silence. His face showed neither pleasure nor annoyance.

'And you are going back to China, Mr Taylor?'

'Yes, sir. God willing!'

'For good?'

'Well, that is the plan.'

'I see. Then I must think upon it, Mr Taylor. I must think upon it.'

'Yes, sir! Of course!'

So, William Faulding thought upon it. And so did Harriett his wife. Mr Faulding might have been persuaded to accept the proposal, but his wife strongly opposed it from the beginning. This was presumably because she knew that Hudson was committed to China full term, and she did not want her daughter lost to her forever.

Jennie begged her mother to approve. Hudson tried more gentle methods on her father. But Mrs Faulding continued to oppose the union with a passion.

William Faulding was a little more sympathetic. He summoned

Hudson to his office and Hudson duly paid him a visit.

As Hudson entered the office, Faulding greeted him rather formally and they shook hands. 'Sit down, Mr Taylor. Please sit down.'

Hudson did. But Faulding did not. He paced the room with his hands behind his back, as if weighing up a difficult problem. Suddenly he stopped.

'We would like you to delay your sailing back to China for a year.'

'Delay it? For a year?'

'Yes, delay it for a year. We'll then allow you to marry our daughter.'

'But I can't do that. I hope to be returning in a few months' time.'

'Those are my terms.' It was spoken like a business deal.

Hudson Taylor left Faulding's office that day crestfallen. His plan was to marry Jennie in the next week or so and to return to China a few months later. Both matters now appeared out of the question.

He met Jennie a little later and they discussed what to do. It was agreed that Hudson would send a letter to Mr Faulding appealing for him to allow them to marry earlier. Jennie suggested some of the wording and she even wrote a second copy of it for them to keep. The letter ended: 'Do not longer withhold your consent.'

What then occurred behind the scenes in the Faulding household must forever be unknown, but, judging by results, it seems probable that William Faulding persuaded his wife to change her mind. A few days later he agreed to an early wedding. It was held on November 28 at Regent's Park Chapel, the church the Fauldings attended. Soon after the wedding the Taylor family moved from Mildmay Road to nearby Pyrland Road.

***

When William Berger finally resigned in March 1872, Hudson Taylor decided to strengthen the home base. Richard Hill and George Soltau agreed to act as Honorary Secretaries, to lead the Mission's affairs in

Britain. Hill was a civil engineer and lay evangelist. Soltau ran a mission in London. Both belonged to the Plymouth Brethren.

Hudson also gained the support of 20 'referees' whose job it would be to promote the CIM cause throughout Britain. These included many significant people from different denominations, including Henry Varley, Lord Radstock and Grattan Guinness, who were all lay evangelists; clergy such as William Pennefather (Anglican) and William Landels (Baptist); and George Müller and Thomas Barnardo, famed for their work on behalf of orphans. Barnardo, in fact, had originally intended to go to China as a missionary, but was so stirred by the plight of London's orphans, that he decided to commit his life to that work instead.

To have such people working at home for the CIM assured a strong base, with widespread support. It also shows that Hudson Taylor was now becoming a much-respected figure in missionary enterprise.

The enlisting of new recruits continued. In September 1872 George and Anne Crombie, who had been on furlough in Britain, returned to China, with Lanfeng and two new missionaries: Fanny Wilson and another lady by the name of Potter. More would soon follow.

The Taylors did not leave England until October 9. They had been in Britain for more than a year, longer than originally planned, though not quite as long as the Fauldings had hoped. They were accompanied on the return trip by another new CIM missionary, Emmeline Turner. The Taylor children were left in England in the care of Emily Blatchley.

CHAPTER 17

MORE TENSIONS, MORE BLESSINGS

'The price in disease and death seemed never ending' (A.J. Broomhall).

While the Taylors were on their way to China, a new head of state was appointed in that land. On November 15, 1872, Emperor Tongzhi, still only a teenager, unofficially assumed power. He had, in fact, been the Emperor since he was five, but up until this time his mother had ruled as regent. It was not until early the following year that he officially took control of China. It was hoped by many that his rule would restore the Qing dynasty and bring order to the land, however he proved difficult to get on with. He argued with the European delegates and later with his own leaders. He died from smallpox early in 1875, before reaching the age of 19. All this added to China's turmoil.

***

The Taylors arrived in Shanghai on 28 November, their first wedding anniversary. Jennie at this stage was more than four months pregnant.

Their first move was to go to the post office to collect their mail. When they arrived there Jennie noticed a figure she recognised. 'Look,' she said, 'there's Charles Fishe.'

Charles Fishe had been sent out to China by CIM in 1868, and became that movement's Chinese secretary three years later. His older brother Edward had preceded him by a year, but had travelled independently and only joined CIM later.

There was Charles in the post office, and dressed in European clothing. When he saw the Taylors he smiled awkwardly. 'Welcome back! Welcome back! Congratulations on your marriage.'

'Thank you!' said Hudson. He thought of making a comment about Fishe's dress, but as, at that moment, he too was clothed in European attire he thought better of it. Instead he asked, 'What's the news? How are things progressing?'

'We have some problems, I fear. We're almost out of money, and the authorities are making life difficult in Hangchow. There's sickness. And a resignation too!'

'Oh! I see. You had better get me up-to-date quickly.'

The two men met formally that evening and discussed the major issues. By the time they had concluded Hudson had already devised a plan.

'Jennie and I will go to Hangchow at the earliest,' he said. 'We'll take Miss Turner and Miss Potter with us. That'll break them in quickly.'

'Yes, Hudson. And what about the money?'

'Well, it may just be there's a mix up in the system somewhere. I'll write to headquarters in London and see what the problem is.' Hudson paused. 'Anyway, I have a little. We can use that.'

Hudson sent the letter and arranged for his visit to Hangchow. They arrived there on December 5 and met Wang, who was still responsible for the church in that region, and in Hudson's estimate 'a wise as well as a godly man.'

'God bless you, Wang. What news? How's the work progressing?'

'Most well, Mr. Taylor. Most well! More conversions, though some backsliders. But God is blessing us. Our evangelists and colporteurs have ventured into Lansi and Anhwei. But come. Let me get you settled for your stay. And some food!'

'Yes, thank you, Wang. There are four of us, though Miss Potter is unwell, I'm afraid.'

They stayed in Hangchow for three weeks. Hudson spent most of that time teaching the Christians and evangelising. While he was there he received cheques valued at nearly £500 from a fund operated by George Müller. That went a long way towards resolving the immediate financial problems.

A little later Miss Potter, whose Christian name seems to have escaped the records, was sent back to England because of her poor health. She died soon afterwards.

But early the next year Hudson decided to settle in Nanking in Kiangsu province. Nanking had proved a difficult place to work, strongly resistant to the Gospel. Hudson thought that he ought to be with Jennie during the final stages of her pregnancy and during the confinement, and if he was to station himself in one place during that time, Nanking seemed a challenging option. It was also central to many other CIM stations.

He also brought Charles Fishe with him. Charles was still wearing European clothes, but Hudson had a high regard for him, describing him as a 'young and devoted missionary.' He was also an able administrator, so was well placed to relieve Hudson of much of the office work.

On the morning of April 12 Jennie went into labour. It proved a most difficult birth. After 24 hours Hudson was so concerned that he called in a doctor based at the Nanking arsenal to help him. But soon after his arrival Jennie started to convulse, became incoherent and failed to recognise Hudson. Early that second afternoon Jennie gave birth. The little boy was stillborn.

Soon after the birth the doctor left to attend to his other duties. Hudson looked after Jennie and nursed his own grief. It was not until the next day that Jennie went into labour again. Jennie gave birth for a second time on the third afternoon. The little girl was also stillborn.

Jennie recovered remarkably quickly. Soon after the birth of her stillborn twins she wrote to her mother, telling her 'It was an intensely anxious time for Hudson.' She failed to mention that it was an intensely terrible time for her.

Jennie was well enough by mid-July that year to accompany Hudson on a brief journey inland along the Yangtze River. This trip was partly exploratory and partly to support existing CIM outposts. Along the way they met Mr Tsiu, now faithfully serving in Tatong in the Shansi province. He still bore the facial scars of his fearful punishment.

When they arrived back news awaited them, mainly of the work in the south. And most of it was bad. William and Mary Rudland were in conflict with their Chinese evangelists and were considering resigning from CIM. Edward Fishe, the brother of Charles, was also talking about resigning to become an independent missionary. One female missionary was so overcome by the difficulties of life in China that she was trying to persuade her husband to go back to Britain; the wife of Wang Lae-djun was dangerously ill; and two missionary wives were experiencing difficult pregnancies.

This would have been enough to discourage most people, but in a strange way it encouraged Hudson Taylor. He wrote at this time, 'Now what do all these things indicate? I think that Satan sees the spreading of the work, dreads it, and is making a strong effort to uproot it. But he will fail. The Lord who is with us is stronger than he.' It was spiritual warfare at its most intense and Hudson Taylor recognised it. 'Oh, for a baptism of the Holy Ghost, the only remedy for our troubles.'

In September, he began a sequence of visits that went on to the end of the year. But first it was to the southern stations to try to heal the rifts and to plan. He had decided to offer Edward Fishe a supporting role, rather than one in the front line.

When they met, Fishe was rather defensive. He shook hands with Hudson, but there was little warmth in it.

'Edward, I've an idea that might appeal to you. Would you be willing to go to Shanghai and supervise the work there? To be our agent, I mean, to supervise incoming missionaries, the mail, the printing press, buy supplies, that sort of thing.'

Fishe visibly softened but was slow in responding. Finally, he said 'Yes, that might be a good idea. I'd be willing to do that.'

A little later Fishe went to Shanghai and began to exercise an efficient administration. That was one problem solved. Hudson also had discussions with the Rudlands, who softened their stand and agreed to continue with CIM. However, Hudson realised they had been in China for over seven years and were clearly in need of a break, so he decided to send them back to Britain for a while.

Hudson also attended two of the female missionaries in their confinements and probably was responsible for saving their lives, though one of the babies was stillborn.

On the financial front matters were still difficult. There barely seemed enough funds to keep existing work going and none for expansion. At this stage CIM had about 100 European and Chinese staff in the field, plus children, and houses, chapels and schools to pay for and maintain.

Jennie had been guaranteed a considerable legacy from a rich uncle who had died in Australia in 1868, and she had decided that when she received it she would give it to the Mission. However, at this stage she was only receiving interest on the sum and no one knew when the full amount was likely to be paid. Yet Hudson still firmly believed that God would provide for their needs, and he even had faith to pray for more missionaries, whom he knew would add to this financial burden. Now Hudson had the vision of entering nine more inland Chinese provinces and he was looking for 18 new missionaries, who would go in two by two. But little by little God did provide.

In the summer of 1874 Hudson and Jennie Taylor left China to return to England, arriving in the middle of October. Some weeks earlier, Hudson had been badly injured in a fall in China and was still hobbling on crutches. The Rudlands and their children, who had recently all had smallpox and recovered from it, went with them. However, eight days after their arrival in Britain Mary Rudland died.

**

Emily Blatchley died on 25 July 1874. She had been ill ever since her time in China. Emily had not only looked after the Taylor children in England, she had also proved to be a most able and helpful correspondent for the CIM. In addition, she wrote poetry, some of which appeared in CIM publications. In the last couple of years Hudson Taylor had relied on her to keep him up-to-date with information from Britain. Hudson, knowing that she was dying, had already sent Louise Desgraz, of the original CIM party, back to England to replace her. Hudson had a high opinion of Desgraz. He believed that few equalled her 'for perseverance in spite of difficulties and discouragements.'

CHAPTER 18

THE WORK ESTABLISHED

'From 1876-1880 Mr Taylor's advent was like a bombshell scattering us' (Elizabeth Wilson).

Hudson Taylor was seriously ill from late 1874 and through the early weeks of 1875. The fall he had had in China proved more devastating than first supposed. His spine was injured and during this period he was in considerable pain and his mobility was severely restricted.

Jennie was pregnant again and nearing full term. At this time, she was sleeping in a room with a missionary candidate named Annie Knight. (It had been decided that it was best for Hudson to sleep in another room because of his and her condition.) One morning Annie was up and about; Jennie was awake but still in bed.

'There's the bell, Mrs Taylor. Breakfast must be ready.'

Jennie moved a little, but did not attempt to get up. 'You go, Annie. I think I'll give breakfast a miss today.'

'Oh! Right! I'll go down then.'

So, Annie descended the stairs to join the others for the meal. Hudson was served breakfast alone in his upstairs room.

Suddenly Jennie began to experience labour pains. *Is this the real thing?* she wondered. *It's a bit early.*

She decided not to call anyone yet, as she thought it too soon. She lay there as each spasm hit.

They are becoming more frequent she thought. *What shall I do?* She decided to do nothing. Yet!

Meanwhile the household had finished breakfast. They all went upstairs and assembled in Hudson's room for prayers. Little Maria Taylor stayed for a while, but then decided to pay Jennie a visit. She tip-toed out of her father's room and then walked along the corridor to where her step-mother was. Along the way she heard some strange, rather frightening noises coming from Jennie. When Maria entered the room, Jennie cried out as another spasm hit. Maria's mouth fell open.

'Mama!' Maria shouted.

'It's the baby.' She let out another groan. 'Get Miss Desgraz. Quickly!'

Maria rushed off to where the others were praying. 'It's the baby. It's the baby!'

All heads lifted. All eyes opened.

'Miss Desgraz, Mama needs you at once.'

Hudson made as if to get up, but was unable to do so.

Louise dashed to the other room where Jennie was now in the later stages of labour. Within minutes the baby boy was born.

When Louise Desgraz had tended to the baby and to Jennie she returned to Hudson's room. His face was anxious. The thought of Jennie's tragic previous delivery had remained etched in his mind.

'How is she? Is she alright? And the baby?'

'Yes, Mr Taylor, she seems well.' Louise said calmly. 'And you have another healthy son.'

'Praise God! Praise God!' Tears of relief began to pour down his cheeks. 'I must see them. You must take me to them.'

'That's not possible, Mr Taylor. Not in your condition!'

'But I must see them. I must.' Hudson looked around the room. 'That small sofa over there. It's mobile, isn't it?'

'I think so.'

'Then wheel it over to the bed and help me on to it.'

Louise looked at the sofa and then back at Hudson Taylor. *This is not going to be easy* she thought. 'Alright! Let's try that.'

She pushed the sofa to the side of the bed and, with difficulty, helped Hudson Taylor on to it. He yelled out in pain as he made the move. She then pushed the sofa with him on it to Jennie's room. He could not stand or even move much, but he did his best to attend to his wife. And then he stared at his newborn son with gratitude to God. The effort had exhausted him, and Louise wheeled him back to his room and helped him back onto his bed.

They named the boy Ernest. In time, Hudson was returned to reasonable health and mobility and eighteen months later Jennie gave birth to a daughter, Amy.

***

The CIM had continued to publish its *Occasional Papers* to keep supporters up-to-date with the Mission's progress. But these papers were occasional and not especially appealing. An issue appeared in March 1875, but it did not please Hudson or Jennie Taylor.

'We need something better, Jennie. These papers have served a purpose, but they do not catch the eye. Nor the imagination!'

Jennie smiled 'No, that's true. So what do we need?'

'I was thinking of producing something larger. And on a more regular basis! With illustrations, that sort of thing! Publications like *The Illustrated London News* have those steel engravings. They *would* catch the eye.'

'They'd be more expensive though, wouldn't they?'

'True, but it would get the CIM message over more effectively.'

'And what would we call it?'

'Well, certainly not *Occasional Papers.*'

Jennie laughed. They thought for a moment, then Jennie said,

'You're always talking about "China's millions," so why not "China's Millions and our work among them."'

'Yes!' said Hudson hesitantly. 'Is that a bit long? Why not just "China's Millions?"'

'That's it. "China's Millions" is perfect.'

In July that year the first issue of *China's Millions* was published, with 'and our work among them' used as a subtitle. One main article asked the question 'Why is not a deeper interest felt in China by the people of England and the Church?' From then *China's Millions* became an essential tool in the work of CIM. That phrase became common and was even repeated in the 1898 missionary hymn by Sarah Stock, 'Let the song go round the earth.' Two lines read

> *'China's millions join the strains,*
> *Waft them on to India's plains.'*

***

The retirement of William Berger from CIM's home leadership had left a gap that even the appointment of the London Council had not adequately filled. So, Hudson was on the lookout for a dedicated and able administrator to head up CIM's affairs in Britain. Benjamin Broomhall, Hudson's old friend and brother-in-law, was considering becoming a missionary, but he and his wife had ten children, which made that rather difficult. Broomhall had already given administrative assistance to CIM and in February 1876 he was taken on to the CIM home staff as an administrator, a position that eventually led to him becoming the General Secretary of the Mission.

One by one and two by two, Hudson Taylor recruited new CIM missionaries in Britain and, after basic training, despatched them to China. By early 1876 eighteen more had been selected, though not all had yet been sent.

On May 26, 1876, a major meeting was held in the Mildmay Conference Hall in London to promote and to pray for CIM. That date was the tenth anniversary of the departure of the *Lammermuir* party. At this meeting Hudson said, 'Our coming together on this occasion is a cause for much joy, and yet what a solemn thing it is. What does it mean? It means that there is a living God, who has loved us and pitied us who were once just as needy as the poor Chinese.' He then showed, using the CIM experience, that taking the Gospel into inland China was possible, and challenged the church in Europe and America to respond to the call.

While the Taylors were still in Britain, part of Hudson's dream became a reality. In April 1875, M Henry Taylor (not related to Hudson) entered Honan province with a Chinese Christian named Zhang. Honan was the first of 'the nine' as yet unevangelised Chinese provinces that CIM entered. Honan, to the centre and north of the country, had a population of about 25 million at that time, so the two Christians were as two specks of sand upon a beach. Henry Taylor baptised the first Honan converts a year after his arrival in the province.

In June 1875, Charles Judd and two Chinese Christians took the Gospel to Hunan, a central province further to the south. In 1876 a group of missionaries, mainly single women, entered Shensi in the north-west.

On September 8 that year, Hudson left England once more to return to China. Jennie and the children stayed in England. Little Amy was just five weeks old. The separation was painful, but necessary. Soon after his departure he wrote to Jennie saying, "'Lo! I come to do Thy will, O God." This is our one duty, our privilege is it not, darling? To do Thy will – you in staying at home, I in leaving you. Day by day, one hour at a time, let us do our Master's work.' He arrived in Shanghai on October 22. This separation was, in the end, only for a little over a year.

A famine began in 1876 in the north-eastern provinces of Shantung and Shansi, which escalated and spread devastatingly to other provinces in 1877-78. The winter was especially savage. The spring rains were desperately needed to give life to the earth and bring a healthy harvest. But on each spring day the skies remained blue and the sun shone brightly. No rain! The results were catastrophic. Missionaries reported seeing ragged and emaciated people begging on the streets, and dogs and birds eating the human corpses that littered the sides of the roads. Cannibalism became common in some of the worst affected areas.

The Christian response to this disaster was immense compared with the size of the Christian community in China. The CIM was active in each of the two northern provinces mostly impacted by these terrible events, and its members and those of other missions rose to the occasion in giving relief. Some of the personnel of these missions died from the fever that became endemic in the terrible conditions. On Hudson's next trip to England he helped alert the British churches to the terrible famine in China, and a fund was set up to give financial aid to those suffering in the drought-affected land.

Hudson Taylor's next visit to Britain, in fact, was late in 1877. He arrived in England five days before Christmas Day. As he travelled on the last few days of the sea journey he thought much about Jennie. *Meeting her again will seem strange after 14 months apart. How will she feel about me? How will I feel about her?* Towards the end of the journey he sent her a note, which said in part, 'May the Lord Jesus not be less to you when I am with you again.' He decided that it would be best for their first meeting to be private, not public.

His children, too, all would be more grown up, all a little different. He wondered, *How will they respond to me?* By this time Herbert Taylor was at medical school and Howard, 19 months younger, was keen to join him when old enough. And China was beckoning to both brothers. Maria was nearly 11, Charles nine, Ernest nearly three and Amy one.

When Hudson and Jennie were reunited it was as if they fell in love again. If 'parting is such sweet sorrow,' reunion brought a far greater sweetness.

Hudson was ill in the middle of the year and Sir Thomas Beauchamp, a rich supporter, invited him to join the Beauchamps on a holiday in Switzerland and the South of France, for Hudson's health. Yet Taylor's attitude to even that was a little unusual. 'I am here for work,' he said, 'the work of getting well again.' All his life was geared to serve God. Fortunately, he found the 'pure air from pure white peaks' exhilarating and his health did improve.

Hudson was away from China for 14 months on this occasion and he continued to arouse interest in taking the Gospel to that land. He spoke enthusiastically at meetings around Britain, focussing on the spiritual needs of the Chinese. It proved a fruitful time. In 1878, 14 men and 14 women joined the Mission and were despatched to China. Four more went in March 1879 and another two that November. This made it possible for the CIM to reach more of the 'nine' provinces.

The comings and goings of the Taylor family continued into the 1880s. Hudson arrived back in China on 22 April 1879. Jennie had already preceded him. Hudson and Maria's eldest son, Herbert, had caught their vision, and in January 1881, before he had turned 20, he left Britain to go to China as a medical missionary. Then Jennie returned to Britain late in 1881, because of the illness of some members of her family. She arrived in Britain on the first day of December. Once more Hudson Taylor was alone.

CHAPTER 19

THE CAMBRIDGE SEVEN

'China is not to be won for Christ by quiet, ease-loving men and women' (Hudson Taylor).

On 6 February 1883 Hudson Taylor left China to return to Britain once more, with the aim of recruiting 70 new workers for the Chinese mission field. Some in CIM thought this too ambitious, at least financially. As so often before, it was proving difficult to raise sufficient funds to support the workers already in China. They wondered, *How would we be able to support another 70?* Benjamin Broomhall, as General Secretary of CIM, had already carried out some of the recruiting. As many as 20 of Broomhall's contacts, including his own son and daughter, were considering going to China. But there was a genuine problem with finance. Yet Hudson Taylor had complete faith that God would provide for 70, 80 or even 100 more.

His other reason for this trip was naturally to see Jennie and his children again. He had not seen her for nearly eighteen months and he had not seen the children who had remained in England for four years. Such long separations were extremely painful. His first footsteps on European soil on this trip were in France. His ship landed at Marseilles on 17 March. He stayed there with a friend for a few days and then caught a train to Paris. Jennie, eager to see him again, went to Paris to meet him.

The train pulled in to the Gare de Lyon. Hudson stepped from the carriage and assembled his luggage. He stood for a moment looking for

Jennie, but could not see her.

Suddenly he saw a figure running towards him. It was Jennie. She rushed into his arms and they kissed. To hold each other again was divine. But they had so much to tell each other, they kept speaking at the same time. Then both stopped and there was silence. They laughed.

Hudson and Jennie carried the luggage outside the station and hailed a cab. They climbed aboard the horse-drawn vehicle and instructed the driver to go to the hotel where Jennie had already booked a room. Strangely, in the cab their talking ceased. Those moments seemed too precious to spoil with chatter. They just sat holding hands, until they arrived at the hotel, where they stayed for a blissful weekend.

But Hudson longed to see his children too, and could never be away from the work in one form or another for long, so on 27 March they went to London. He was overwhelmed when he saw them. Tears came to his eyes. He shook hands warmly with Howard, a grown man, and embraced an excited Maria. He soon discovered that they had grown into fine Christians. By this time Howard was 20, full of energy and, as hoped, continuing his medical studies. Maria was 16 and already keen to go to China. (Maria Taylor went to China in 1884 at the age of 17, and Howard, after 'acquiring high academic distinction in medicine and surgery' in 1888, aged 25.)

Hudson next went to CIM Headquarters to see Benjamin Broomhall and to check on the Mission's affairs at first hand. Broomhall greeted him warmly. 'Welcome home, Hudson! Welcome home!'

Hudson smiled. 'I'm not quite sure where home is nowadays. Perhaps it's China. How are things going? Is our financial situation as bad as some are saying?'

Broomhall hesitated for a moment. 'Well, Hudson,' he eventually said, 'we are not flush with funds, but God is blessing us and we always seem to have enough to meet our expenses. However, we certainly haven't enough to send another 70 to China. But I believe God will supply our needs.'

'Yes, praise Him, He will.'

'We have a much higher profile now, too.'

'Higher profile?'

'Yes! The Mission is much better known now and we're receiving funds from around the country. We've a lot of support.'

The two men discussed the Mission's affairs in depth: staff on the field, candidates preparing to go and finance. Hudson discovered that the CIM was in good hands at its British headquarters. He was most impressed by the energetic work that Broomhall was doing as General Secretary. Broomhall was a dedicated man and a good organiser.

***

Amongst the eventual recruits that Hudson Taylor enlisted on this trip were seven talented young men from privileged backgrounds who became known as the Cambridge Seven. That name derived from the belief that each of the Seven had been to Cambridge University, though in fact only six of them had. The Seven were C. T. (Charlie) Studd, Stanley Smith, Montagu Beauchamp (son of Sir Thomas), William Cassels, Dixon (Dick) Hoste and two brothers, Arthur and Cecil Polhill-Turner.

They were a remarkable collection of missionary candidates. Charlie Studd was famous as one of three cricketing brothers. He had played in the original 'Ashes' Test at the Kennington Oval in August 1882, and, with one of his brothers, George, was in the touring party to Australia a few months later, which regained the 'Ashes.' (Twenty years later George Studd became involved in the famous Azusa Street Mission.)

Studd's mother had been strongly opposed to her son going to China. She paid Jennie Taylor a visit in London, presumably to try to get her to persuade Hudson not to take him. But whatever transpired between the two women Mrs Studd eventually accepted the inevitable.

Stanley Smith was the son of a well-known London surgeon. He was another sporting hero. One of the major sporting events in the British calendar was the Oxford and Cambridge boat race held on the River Thames. Smith, a tall and powerful man, had rowed stroke for the Cambridge crew in that race.

Smith had also helped in the D. L. Moody evangelistic campaign in London early in 1884 and was considering joining Moody to train new converts. After one evangelistic meeting Smith was invited to a dinner party. One of the other guests was Hudson Taylor. After the dinner Smith went for a walk with Taylor, who told him about the work in China. By the end of the evening Smith had decided to go to China with the CIM.

Montagu Beauchamp's family had earlier befriended Hudson Taylor. They had met him many years ago, and had renewed their acquaintance with him in recent times on his holiday in Switzerland and France. Montagu had become a deacon in the Church of England. He had heard of Studd's determination to go to China, despite family opposition, and had been deeply impressed by it. These factors were primary motivators behind his decision to go to China.

William Cassels had attended St John's College, Cambridge, and had already been ordained into the Church of England ministry. He was at that time curate at All Saints Church in South Lambeth, London, a highly successful working-class parish. He was a quiet man and nicknamed 'William the Silent'.

When Cassels told his mother that he was hoping to go to China with CIM, she was heartbroken. Mrs Cassels had seven sons and six of them were already overseas. She was very reluctant to let go of the seventh. She wrote a letter to Hudson Taylor pleading with him not to take her son away.

This put Hudson in a difficult position. He needed reinforcements in China, Cassels was a good candidate and willing to go, but Taylor could not ignore this woman's plea. He wrote back a carefully worded letter saying, 'I hold a parent's wishes sacred, and I will not encourage William to join CIM if you oppose it.' Fortunately, soon afterwards she wrote another letter to Taylor removing her objection, saying, 'If I tried to stop him going, I would be a bad mother to the best of sons.'

This highlights the terrible difficulty that the parents of missionaries faced in the nineteenth century. Travel was slow, communications poor and disease always a danger. It was not easy for parents to see their children go off into the unknown, knowing full well that they might never see them again.

Dixon Hoste was the one of the Seven who had not been to Cambridge University, though his brother had. He was a Lieutenant in the Royal Artillery, and the son of a Major-General. Like Cassels, Dixon was quiet and shy. He was the first of this group to contact CIM about serving in China.

Then there were the Polhill-Turner brothers. Arthur Polhill-Turner had been converted through earlier meetings held by D. L. Moody in Cambridge. These had been organised by Kynaston Studd, the eldest brother of Charlie Studd. Arthur's brother Cecil was another officer in the British Army. They were sons of a Captain in the 6th Dragoon Guards who became a Member of Parliament and High Sheriff of Bedfordshire.

Arthur Polhill-Turner was the youngest of the Seven. At the time of their departure for China he was only 21. All of them were under 26 and each of these men had rank or position in society. They all came from favoured backgrounds. But Hudson Taylor did not primarily choose them because of such matters. He was too smart for that. Rather he chose them because they were all dedicated to the cause of Christ and, he believed, could forward that cause in China. He knew, though, that they would make good leaders.

That these men had decided to join Hudson Taylor in taking the

Gospel to the Chinese clearly indicates how highly Taylor was now viewed by the Christian public. He was a man highly respected, even revered.

When the Christian community in Britain became aware that these men had signed on as CIM missionaries, this further widened and deepened the interest in CIM. Hudson Taylor was fast becoming aware of that and in October 1884 he approached Broomhall about aiming higher than the original 70 extra candidates.

'What do you think, Benjamin? We have that 70 now and the interest is still growing. Should we look for another 70, and another?'

Broomhall smiled. 'Hold on, Hudson. Not quite so fast. Let's assess our situation before we set any more goals.'

'But if we have already gained seven Cambridge men, why not more like them? I'm not saying that we should look only for the well-educated, but such men will make excellent leaders in the field. And if Cambridge, why not Oxford!'

Broomhall smiled again. 'But how can we do that?'

'What if we send, say, Smith, Studd and Beauchamp to Oxford and Cambridge to stir up interest? They have the contacts. They are respected by their peers. Let's give it a try.'

Broomhall thought for a moment, and then in little more than a whisper said, 'Why not?'

In November Hudson Taylor sent Studd, Smith and Hoste to conduct a recruiting campaign in Oxford. Beauchamp was not available for this visit.

'Into the enemy camp, eh Charlie?' said Smith with a laugh.

'Yes, it is rather like that. I would find it easier to play them on the cricket field.'

Smith laughed again. 'Or on the Thames!'

They all laughed. However, whatever feelings they may have had they went to Oxford and held a series of meetings scattered over the next six days. Sadly, they were poorly attended. Perhaps that was because Oxford had a different ethos from Cambridge. Perhaps it was because of inter-university rivalry. But whatever the reason, disheartened by their apparent failure, they travelled to Cambridge, minus Hoste, but with the addition of Montagu Beauchamp.

Though their trip to Oxford had met with little success, it proved very different in Cambridge. They were received like royalty, speaking in various halls packed with enthusiastic men and women. Hudson Taylor led the charge, introducing the trio one by one at each venue, though not all spoke at every meeting.

At one meeting on the second Sunday in Cambridge, Hudson Taylor and Stanley Smith each spoke. Before the close of the meeting Taylor asked any who wished to serve overseas to stand. Fifty did so. After the final meeting forty-five enquired about missionary service. Helpers took down the names of these volunteers.

Suddenly a missionary enterprise became big news. The Press, secular as well as religious, took notice of these events and reported them widely. That seven young men with wealth, learning and great potential, should all lay aside material prosperity to serve Christ in China captured the public's imagination. The ex-Cambridge men were first dubbed 'the spiritual millionaires'. They were men of wealth and rank, but this they considered of little account compared with the riches found in Jesus Christ.

Hudson Taylor began to receive many more calls from churches and organisations in England and Scotland for missionary speakers, so he decided to use Studd, Smith and their companions to fulfil these requests. Taylor dispatched Studd, Smith and R. J. Landale, an already established CIM missionary, to Edinburgh University to stir up the interest there, in a campaign that proved very successful.

Such was the clamour to hear the Cambridge Seven that Hudson

Taylor agreed to postpone their departure for a few weeks, until early February. He then sent his would-be missionaries on a whistle-stop tour of Britain in the second half of January, with the dual purpose of proclaiming the Gospel and encouraging others to enlist for missionary service.

Hudson, however, did not see the fruits of those meetings firsthand. He left to return to China in the middle of January and arrived in Shanghai early in March. He then prepared the way for the Seven and those whom he knew would soon follow them. The CIM was growing and advancing, but Hudson knew that the task ahead for them was too big for them alone and full of difficulties.

After Hudson Taylor had departed, Studd and Smith went on a preaching tour, supported by the well-known independent evangelist Reginald Radcliffe. They visited Liverpool, and Edinburgh again, before returning to England, speaking in Newcastle, Manchester, Rochdale and Leeds. They spoke in halls and churches to packed and enthusiastic crowds, with some coming to faith in Christ and others offering to serve Christ overseas.

They visited Liverpool again on 29 January and then returned to London. The official farewell to the Cambridge Seven was to be held the next day at the Eccleston Hall. Yet even after this there were further invitations to speak in Bristol, Oxford and Cambridge, further delaying their departure.

A final meeting was then scheduled for 4 February 1885 at the Exeter Hall, which held over 4,000. It was wet and cold, the kind of winter's day one would like to forget, yet the hall was packed. It was to prove memorable for the seven young men and the thousands who gathered to hear them.

Upon the platform sat no less than 40 Cambridge graduates who had volunteered for missionary service, and behind them was a massive map of China, making clear the purpose of the gathering. At the proposed commencement time the Seven filed on to the platform, led by Smith, and were greeted with the now customary cheers and applause.

George Williams of the YMCA, who was chairing the meeting, held up his hand and gradually the commotion ceased. Williams announced a hymn and the hall erupted into song. Canon Stevenson prayed and Williams addressed the crowd. 'Many years ago our gracious Queen said that the Bible was the source of England's greatness. And so it is. So, we are pleased to give each of these gentlemen a Bible in Chinese, with the hope that what the Bible has done for Great Britain it will also do for China. These Bibles are being presented on behalf of the British and Foreign Bible Society.' As each Bible was presented more applause thundered through the auditorium.

When the noise quietened down Williams said, 'Ladies and Gentlemen, I would like to introduce you to Mr Benjamin Broomhall, the General Secretary of the China Inland Mission.'

Benjamin Broomhall rose to speak to the audience. 'This is a remarkable occasion,' he began. 'A most exciting venture! It was a mere 20 years ago that the China Inland Mission was formed by Hudson Taylor. It arose out of his great concern that there were so few missionaries in China amidst such a vast mass of people. So few to take the good news of Christ to the Chinese. The Mission's abiding principle was from the beginning to accept people of any denomination, providing they believed the teachings of the Bible. The doctrines of the Evangelical Alliance became our standard. Since then many have gone out and the work of Christ has moved into the heart of China. But still there are so few missionaries amongst so many.

'It is, therefore, wonderful to be able to send these seven gentlemen off tonight.' Applause broke out again. Broomhall held up his hand for silence, and then continued, 'In a moment you will hear from each one, and you will hear how they are all dedicated to the task of taking the Gospel to the Chinese. Whatever the difficulties, whatever the dangers, these men will play their part. They will brave the dangers and overcome the difficulties to win China for Christ.

'Yet these seven are not alone. Others have gone before them and more are here on the platform who will go soon.' He extended his hand towards the group assembled behind him. Applause broke out again. 'Yet more are still needed. Is God calling you to this great work?

'Let me introduce you to these seven men. Each will give you a brief account of their call to the mission field. First, Mr Stanley Smith!'

Smith rose from his seat, moved to the front of the platform to cheers and applause and addressed the crowd. Each of the others took their turn and spoke briefly.

The next day the Seven assembled at Victoria Station to catch the boat train. When the Cambridge Seven arrived in Shanghai the CIM had about 150 missionaries in the field.

The extraordinary publicity generated by the calling of these eminent young men raised the profiles of Hudson Taylor and the CIM considerably. It also further boosted the number of missionary candidates, not only for CIM, but also for other missionary societies in Britain. As Benjamin Broomhall later said, 'In that final week the China Inland Mission had been suddenly lifted into unusual and unexpected prominence and even popularity.' But he warned 'The hour of success is often the time of danger, a snare and not a blessing.'

To celebrate the departure of the Seven, CIM published a special edition of *China's Millions*; the print run of 50,000 quickly sold out. It was later produced in book form with considerable additional material. This ran to three editions and sold 20,000 copies.

CHAPTER 20

RETURN TO CHINA

'A hand to hand conflict with the powers of darkness' (Hudson Taylor).

While Hudson Taylor had been in Britain on the recent trip there had been more turmoil in China, including some attacks on Christians. At the end of 1883 and the beginning of the following year about 18 Protestant chapels had been destroyed. In August 1884, a French fleet destroyed many Chinese vessels and blockaded Taiwan. Not surprisingly, this infuriated many Chinese, who attacked anything considered western, including Christians, Chinese and European, Protestant and, especially, Catholic. Being a Christian in China was not getting easier.

***

The Cambridge Seven had become a team; a team, in the popular mind in England at least, who were going to play 'the game' of missionary life together, taking the Gospel to the Chinese. However, it was clear that with the limited resources at his disposal, Hudson Taylor would need to break up this group and send them to different locations. Hudson decided that the best plan was, first, to help them become familiar with China and its ways and to improve their language skills. Then he planned to despatch them to three separate destinations.

Charles Studd and the Polhill brothers were to join the work in Hanchung, over 1,500 kilometres away to the north-west. Smith was due to go with Cassels and Hoste north to Shansi, while it was Hudson Taylor's plan to take Beauchamp with him on his own travels. As his departure was not to be immediate, he decided to let Beauchamp go part of the way with Studd and his companions, so that he would gain some experience of inland China, and then to return to Shanghai. However, when Beauchamp returned, Hudson had become so busy with administrative matters that he had to cancel his planned trip. He then decided to send Beauchamp north in the company of an experienced missionary to join Smith, Cassels and Hoste.

On the way north, Studd and the Polhills found language study too laborious and decided to adopt 'the biblical way' and prayed for the gift of tongues. When they arrived in Hanchung they were still praying for that and encouraged two female missionaries to do the same. Nothing happened, so it was back to the books.

Hudson Taylor was most upset when he heard about it. He wrote, 'How many and subtle are the devices of Satan to keep the Chinese ignorant of the Gospel. If I could put the Chinese language into your brains by one wave of the hand, I would not do it.' He believed that learning the language through teachers skilled in the intricacies of the language and culture was essential for all the CIM workers, however hard it might be.

Stanley Smith, a most able speaker in English, proved to be the quickest and most capable of the Seven in learning Chinese. It was not long before he was holding the rapt attention of Chinese audiences.

***

Early in May, Hudson left Shanghai and travelled along the canal to Kiangsi province, a little to the west. He had explored this area before and a work had begun there, but he was keen to strengthen it. He took with him his son, Herbert, John McCarthy (an early CIM missionary), Mariamne [sic] Murray and her sister Cecilia, Jeanie Gray, Mary

Williams and, eventually, Kate Macintosh. They travelled in two boats, the men in one and the women in the other.

It was Hudson's intention to establish mission stations to evangelise along the Guangzin River, which ran through Kiangsi. Before they reached their destination McCarthy and Hudson left them to visit another mission station. This left Herbert Taylor with the four women. Inevitably, he fell in love with one of them, Jeanie Gray. But, as so often in mission work, they were soon to be separated.

Hudson rejoined the group, and as they visited various communities he noticed how well many of the Chinese responded to the women. He decided to post Jeanie and Kate at Yushan, near the eastern border of Kiangsi. They would live in the home of a Chinese Christian couple, and base their activities there. Sending unmarried women into the interior of China was an unconventional move by Taylor, but it was so successful that the church in Yushan grew from 30 to over 100 in a year. When Jeanie Gray left to marry Herbert Taylor, Mary Williams replaced her.

Hudson was delighted with the successful experiment and placed other young women in pairs in strategic places along the Guangzin River. After their marriage Herbert and Jeanie settled in Dagutang by Poyang Lake in the western region of Kiangsi. John McCarthy acted as overall supervisor of these stations.

With the enlarging CIM workforce it was inevitable that Hudson Taylor had to increase the amount of time he spent on administration. However much others assisted him in this he still had to be heavily involved in the distribution of staff, and he usually had the last word (and often the first word) about policy. There was much mail, going in and out, some of which demanded his attention. He also had to be at least aware of the financial situation, and funds were rarely plentiful. He could not keep up with it all. It seemed to him that, 'The carrots go ahead however fast the donkey runs.'

To ease his administrative burdens, in January 1886 he appointed James Broumton, a long serving CIM missionary, as Treasurer of the Mission in China. Two months later he appointed John Stevenson, recently returned from furlough, Deputy Director of the Mission in China.

***

In this period there were successes and failures. Some provinces more readily accepted the Christian message than others.

The province of Hunan in the south had been entered in June 1875, but it proved to be a tough nut to crack. Little progress was made in the following ten years, as there was considerable opposition to anything foreign in that province.

In 1886 Henry Dick and a converted Buddhist priest managed to enter the state capital Changsha. This was remarkable. They may have been allowed in because the guards on the city gate did not immediately realise that Dick, dressed in Chinese clothing, was a European. Once in they were bold enough to go to the mandarin's residence.

They approached the guard on the door and both bowed. Dick's companion said, 'We wish to see the mandarin. We have a wonderful story to tell him about Jesus our Lord. We also have a gift for him.' He pulled a Bible from his bag and gave it to the guard.

The guard scowled, grabbed the Bible and disappeared. About 20 minutes later he returned without the Bible, accompanied by two more guards. All three looked menacing. 'No foreigners here!' shouted the lead guard. 'Mandarin say, "No foreigners here!" Go away.'

Dick and his companion realised that it would be fruitless to argue and backed away. When they reached the street outside, they saw that a threatening crowd had gathered. It moved in on the two men, jostling them and spitting at them. 'Beat the foreigner! Death to the foreigner!' they cried. Fortunately for the two Christians there was more noise than real danger. The crowd, still shouting and screaming, forcibly directed them through the city gate and back to their boat.

Hunan remained a difficult province.

But matters were worse in Chungking in Szechwan province in the far west in the summer of 1886. Cecil Polhill (he had now dropped the Turner part of his name), Edward Pearse and two Chinese Christians, Ho and Liang, approached the city on July 3 and heard disturbing sounds.

'What's the noise?' asked the two Englishmen, almost simultaneously. They looked at Ho and Liang.

'I think there is trouble in the city,' said Ho.

'Trouble?' asked Pearse.

This time Liang responded. 'It sounds dangerous.'

'Then we had better enter carefully,' said Pearse.

The four men looked at each other. Each nodded and they quietly entered the city.

The nature of the 'trouble' quickly became evident. Dozens of young men were in the process of destroying the prominently-situated building owned by the American Episcopal Mission. They were shouting and screaming and smashing furniture, walls and equipment, everything they could find.

The four Christians looked at each other once more. 'What do we do now?' said Polhill quietly.

'I'll try to find out more,' said Ho. He went over to some bystanders and talked with them for a few minutes, and then returned to his companions.

'It's not just here, I'm afraid. Our building has been wrecked too, it seems. And the Catholic Cathedral! All foreigners in the town are in the mandarin's yamen. It's the safest place.'

'That's probably where we should go,' said Pearse.

'Should we go to our house first, do you think?' asked Polhill.

'The trouble-makers aren't there anymore. It might be safe to do so,' said Ho.

'Yes, I suppose we should go and see the damage.' Pearse looked at the mob smashing everything at the American mission. 'It doesn't look too hopeful though.'

So, they quietly made their way to the CIM house. It was still standing. But everything worth stealing had been stolen, and everything else inside had been destroyed. They moved on to the mandarin's residence and were duly admitted. It was two weeks before matters quietened down. Then the mandarin summoned them to appear before him.

'It's time for you to go. Out of Chungking! Out of Szechwan!' he said.

'Out of Szechwan?' Polhill and the others favoured the idea of leaving the city, but not the province.

'Out! Out of Szechwan!' The mandarin was clearly not in the mood for debating the issue. 'We have some boats for you. I will accompany you to them. Then you must go.'

At that the 'foreigners' and their Chinese companions collected their luggage and prepared to leave. The mandarin was true to his word and accompanied them to their vessels.

***

One key Chinese worker was Pastor Hsi, nicknamed 'Shengmo,' which means 'Conqueror of Demons.' He had been raised in a Confucian family and had an enquiring mind, but he became addicted to opium.

David Hill, a Wesleyan missionary, gave him a copy of the New Testament, and he began to read it. Hsi was struck forcibly by the life of Jesus. He read the Gospel accounts over and over again, and through reading them was converted to Christ. Then began a fierce battle against his addiction, in which Hsi, and the Spirit of God in Hsi, was eventually triumphant. The demons had been conquered, for he never took opium again. Shengmo often worked with CIM missionaries including Hudson Taylor and Charlie Studd.

Shansi in the north had been one of the nine unevangelised Chinese provinces of just a few years ago. But Hudson Taylor had sent some of his faithful staff to that state to tell its people of Christ. At the beginning of August 1886, Hudson, accompanied by John Stevenson and Stanley Smith, held a series of meetings for Chinese Christians in the Shansi town Hongtong. Word of the pending meetings had been spread far and wide and Christians from much of south-east Shansi eagerly came together for them. By the time the first meeting was held there were about a hundred men present and almost as many women. Hsi Shengmo was among them. Recent storms had made the roads treacherous, probably keeping many more away.

Hudson Taylor had recently been sick with dysentery, but he was determined not to miss this opportunity. He stood on a specially constructed platform, and as he addressed the gathering he noticed numerous onlookers around the fringes of the courtyard. They were not Christians but had just come out of curiosity.

The sight of all these eager faces beaming up at him sent a thrill down Hudson Taylor's spine. This was the fulfilment of a dream, in part at least. Two hundred Chinese Christians in one place at one time. It was only 25 years ago that there would not have been many more Protestant Christians of Chinese descent in the whole of China.

Hudson spoke on our Lord's words: 'My peace,' 'My joy,' 'My glory,' from verses in John's Gospel. He began with 'Peace I leave with you, *my peace* I give unto you; not as the world giveth, give I unto you. Let not your heart be troubled, neither let it be afraid' (John 14:27). He followed it with 'These things have I spoken unto you, that *my joy* might remain in you, and that your joy might be full' (John 15:11). He ended with 'Father

... that they may behold *my glory*, which thou hast given me' (John 17:24).

In a country in which war and trouble, with a resulting lack of peace and joy, had become all too common, it was a striking message. The crowd sat enthralled. When he had finished speaking some of the onlookers asked the Chinese believers questions about this Jesus.

That evening, at a second meeting, with lanterns flickering around the perimeter of the courtyard, John Stevenson spoke briefly on 'The Kingdom of God is not in words, but in power.' He concluded by saying, 'I would now like to invite any who have experienced that kingdom power in their lives to come up here to the platform to tell us about it.'

The first on his feet was Hsi Shengmo. 'In looking back on my past life' he began, 'I can, indeed, see the guiding hand of God. As a child I remember thinking *What is the use of being in this world? Men find no good.* And I remember crying as I thought of it. My brother urged me to read books, that in so doing I might become a mandarin. *Well,* I thought, *what good is there in becoming a mandarin? Sooner or later I must still die.* And I was afraid to die, and I used to wonder how it could be avoided.'

Hsi went on to tell how he became an opium addict and about the terrible affects it had on his life. Knowing that there were addicts on the fringes of the congregation, he then said, 'But God did what man and medicine could not do. He enabled me to break off smoking opium. My friends, if you would break off opium, don't rely on medicine, don't lean on man, trust in God. And thanks be to God, He saved my soul. Mr Hill led me to the gate. God caused me to enter. My friends, is not this the grace of Jesus?' And so his fear of death was ended.

When Hsi sat down five other Chinese followed, each telling of what Christ had done for them. One told how he had been a soldier. After leaving the army he and his family had been starving during the famine. They were helped by David Hill at this terrible time. He later visited Hill to thank him, and he heard the missionary singing 'Jesus loves me.' *But,* he thought, *he can sing that, but I can't. Jesus doesn't love me.*

When he told Hill his thoughts, the missionary responded, 'Jesus loves not only me but you. Jesus is able to forgive your sins. Don't you ever forget that.'

He did not forget it. He later came to believe in Christ and was baptised. He then became a colporteur, at one time travelling with a missionary through Hunan, the usually non-responsive province, and selling thousands of books.

Hudson closed the meeting by telling a little of his own testimony and concluding, 'God is, indeed, faithful. For 20 years I have laboured and prayed for Shansi. These testimonies are such an encouragement to me. What we have heard today tells of God's great faithfulness in answering prayer and saving souls. Praise His Name!'

On the second day several men and women were ordained to act as pastors, elders and deacons in their respective churches. Hsi Shengmo was appointed 'watcher over and feeder of the sheep of God,' with a travelling ministry. Later, 56 Chinese were baptised, some again testifying to what Christ had done in their lives.

Soon after those meetings Hudson travelled by land south-west to Hanchung with a small group including Montagu Beauchamp, Charlie Studd, Herbert Taylor and some Chinese men. It was hot, very hot. Hudson was still unwell, so they decided to travel by night. While this suited Hudson, the others in the party found it difficult so they split into two groups, Taylor and Beauchamp went by night with two Chinese, the others by day.

While Taylor could easily sleep by day, Beauchamp could not, but they pressed on together. Travelling by night also had its difficulties. If there was a full moon, then there was usually sufficient light, but if there was not, it did become dangerous.

One night they reached a small river. 'Can we wade across this?'

Hudson asked his Chinese companions.

'It's quite deep. The rains have made it deeper than usual. But it's not flowing too quickly,' said one of them.

'I think we can do it,' said the other.

'But I don't think you can, Hudson. Not in your condition,' said Beauchamp.

'Don't worry, old chap. I'll get there.'

'No! I'll carry you.'

'Carry me?'

'Yes! There's no other way.'

So, the Chinese men lifted Hudson onto Beauchamp's shoulders and they began the hazardous crossing. The three men waded through the waist deep water, the two Chinese on either side of Beauchamp, steadying Hudson Taylor every time he looked like he might fall off. They reached the other side, the Chinese helped Hudson down and Beauchamp collapsed on the ground.

'Well done, my friend. I thank you,' said Hudson.

Beauchamp laughed. 'I hope there aren't too many more of those.'

Charlie Studd, Herbert Taylor and the others reached the Yellow River first and waited for Hudson and his party. When they all had assembled they prepared to cross the river, and this was a river that certainly could not be waded. In fact, the Yellow River was 'running high and very dangerous,' but they boarded a ferry, with their luggage. More and more people scrambled aboard, some leading mules and other beasts. Then the boatman prepared to depart.

'I'm not sure this is safe, Father,' said Herbert Taylor.

Hudson looked at the roaring river and the over-loaded boat and said, 'You may be right, Herbert. I think we had better pray.' So they did.

The ferry left the bank, but was swept downstream at a furious pace, colliding with logs and other debris. It spun and rocked in the fast-flowing river. They all held on grimly as the boat made its mad and erratic progress. Getting to the other side quickly became a secondary consideration. Getting to either side at all in safety was the only thing that mattered now.

'Look out! There goes a mule.' Sure enough, a mule fell overboard and was quickly lost in the flood. Then another fell, and another and another! This was bad for the mules, but it turned out to be good for the humans. The animals' unfortunate departure had lightened the load a little and the vessel eventually made it safely to the other side of the river. After resting they marched on to Hanchung.

CHAPTER 21

RAPID EXPANSION

'God's work done in God's way will never lack God's supply' (Hudson Taylor).

Hudson's Taylor's vision was never dimmed. In the two preceding years, he had travelled thousands of kilometres and visited nine of the Chinese provinces, ever extending the work of CIM. In November 1886, he called the leaders of the CIM in China together for a council. They met in Anking in Anhui province, which was in the east of China, but inland from Shanghai. The council began with several days of prayer, upon some of which they all fasted.

The Mission now had 187 missionaries, of which 77 were considered 'experienced.' The others were either novices or, at least, still learning the ropes. Learning Chinese was a problem that they all faced, so it was decided to establish a language school to aid with this. John Stevenson had already drafted an eight-stage course for new missionaries, and Frederick Baller was commissioned to write a Mandarin Primer. The council also worked on producing a booklet of 'Principles and Practice' for the Mission. In a widely-scattered mission field, in which communicating took a long time, this would help everyone to know what was expected and how to deal with problems.

Most importantly the council boldly decided to enlist another 100 missionaries in the next year. It was a daring decision. After 20 years, they had less than 200 people in China, now they were hoping to increase that by more than 50 percent in just one year. Hudson arranged for John Stevenson to write to CIM headquarters in London with this remarkable request. Two days later Hudson further confirmed it when he wrote to Jennie, saying, 'We are praying for 100 new missionaries in 1887. The Lord help in the selection and provide the means.'

Whatever doubts some may have had about this, Hudson was certain that it could be achieved. He said to John Stevenson, 'If you showed me a photograph of the whole 100 taken in China, I could not be more sure than I am now.'

To this end it was agreed that Hudson Taylor had to go to Britain once more. He left on January 6, 1887 and arrived on February 18.

The houses at Pyrland Road, which had so often housed the Taylors and CIM trainees and missionaries, were now proving inadequate for that task. In July a contract was signed on a piece of land in nearby Newington Green on which would be built a new headquarters. A larger building was needed to cope with the increased Mission activity.

With so much administrative work and attempts to find the 100, Hudson was under a great deal of self-applied pressure. Amidst it all, when Hudson paid a visit to Belfast, Jennie wrote to him, saying, 'Do rest before it is too late. It will not pay to kill yourself, even to get the 100.'

But remarkably, by the end of 1887 about 100 new missionaries had been added to the CIM staff. The CIM now had 265 missionaries in China. This was more than twice as many as any other missionary society. The Mission also had 132 Chinese staff. In addition, it had well over 600 churches, three hospitals and 17 homes for opium addicts in China.

By this time, there was growing concern in Britain about the continuing flow of opium into China. Benjamin Broomhall, as well as being a leading figure in the CIM, was on the committee of the Society for the Suppression of the Opium Trade, and, while in England, Hudson

Taylor added his voice to that campaign.

A World Missionary Conference was held in London in 1888, which attracted over 1,500 delegates from Britain and its colonies, continental Europe, and North America. Over 100 missionary societies including CIM were involved in this.

Hudson Taylor attended it and, amongst other matters, moved a resolution condemning the opium trade. Part of it said, 'This Conference … deeply deplores the position occupied by Great Britain, through its Indian administration, in the manufacture of the drug and in the promotion of a trade, which is one huge ministry to vice.' Taylor's resolution went on to urge the government to focus on 'the entire suppression of the trade' and for Christians in Britain to pray and 'give themselves no rest, until this great evil is entirely removed.' The resolution was passed easily, but the Conference committee did not view it favourably, so it did not become official. However, the stand had been taken and Benjamin Broomhall and others continued the fight against British involvement in the trade.

It may seem over-optimistic that missionary societies and the wider Christian community could take on the all-powerful British Government and win. However, three years earlier, in the sensational Maiden Tribute campaign, conducted and supported mainly by Christians, the then government was forced to raise the age of consent for sexual intercourse from 13 to 16. In other words, the British government could be persuaded by public opinion to adopt fairer and more just laws, so this move that Hudson was urging was not unrealistic.

However, British involvement in the opium trade did not end until early in the twentieth century, and that final decision may have had more to do with economics than morality.

***

In July of that year Hudson met Henry Weston Frost, an American. A few years earlier Frost had been in his room at Princeton with a friend who was showing him a revolver that his father had used in the American Civil War. Both men assumed that the gun was not loaded. But it was. As the friend handled the weapon, it went off and a bullet whistled past Frost's ear. Both of them were deeply shocked. As Frost recovered from the experience he came to believe that he had escaped death for a reason.

He became interested in overseas mission and read about the Cambridge Seven. He was greatly impressed by their dedication and heroism. Soon after that he heard Kynaston Studd, a brother of Charlie Studd, speak about the needs of China. Frost began to think about going to China himself, but his health was not good and he also had a sick relative that needed care, so he decided against it. But, as China would not leave his mind, he went to Britain to approach the CIM about opening a branch in America.

He met with Hudson Taylor at the end of 1887. Frost was immediately impressed by Taylor. He later said, 'I had, then and there, what amounted to a revelation – first of a man and then of his God. From that moment my heart was fully his.' He put forward his proposal, but Hudson Taylor and Benjamin Broomhall did not view it favourably. They were overwhelmed by the rapid expansion of the Mission over the last few years, and the numerous difficulties they were facing because of that, including some disagreements in the ranks. A new venture at that time seemed out of the question.

After the matter had been considered, Hudson told Frost, 'I am sorry, Mr Frost, but I cannot see the leading of the Lord to take this step at this time. Perhaps the way ahead would be for you to begin a new mission along the lines of the China Inland Mission.'

Frost was shattered and did not know how to respond. But before he left Britain he approached Hudson with another suggestion.

'Mr Taylor, as I'm sure you know, there are a number of mission conferences held regularly in America, led by Mr Moody and other faithful men. Would you consent to come to America and speak at these conferences?'

It was Hudson's turn this time to be reduced to silence. He had not expected this. After a few moments thought he recovered himself, and said, 'Well, Mr Frost, I might be able to do that. But I must have invitations from the organisers of these conferences.'

Frost's mood lifted. 'Yes, Mr Taylor, that is wonderful. Thank you. Thank you so much. I'm sure I can arrange those invitations.' A day or two later Frost boarded a ship to return to the USA.

When he arrived back in America, Frost quickly contacted two key men in the conference movement, William J. Erdman and Arthur T. Pierson. Pierson was also the editor of *The Missionary Review of the World*. These two lost no time in offering invitations to Hudson Taylor. D. L. Moody also approached Hudson at about the same time. With invitations from such prominent and dedicated figures, Hudson could not say no.

On June 23, 1888, he left England to travel to America and arrived in New York on the first day of July. Amongst his travelling companions were his son Howard, Reginald Radcliffe, an English evangelist, and George Studd.

One of Hudson's first visits was to Northfield, Massachusetts, to speak to Moody's students. He then went to Niagara-on-the-Lake, which was the major site used for the Bible Conferences, where he spoke twice to about 400 people. Strikingly, he did not speak about the CIM and not even about mission generally. His focus was on Jesus Christ. His second address was on 'Have faith in God' and included the immortal words, 'It is not so much great faith that we need, but faith in a great God.' Faith to Hudson Taylor was not an 'airy-fairy' concept, but something real and dynamic and always directed in God through His Son Jesus Christ.

It was next on to bustling Chicago, where he preached in Moody's church. This was the beginning of a whistle-stop tour, which aroused great interest in CIM and a considerable amount of money. But when Hudson heard about the money he was not pleased.

'Is this money to be used for Americans?' he asked Frost.

'Yes, that is the understanding.'

Hudson Taylor frowned. 'This is serious' was all he said.

But his mind was in turmoil. *I have so far opposed establishing a wing of CIM in the USA. But am I now being forced by American generosity to do so?* Then characteristically he said to Frost, 'To have missionaries and no money would not cause me any anxiety. But to have money and no missionaries is a very serious matter.'

Frost was stunned into silence by this comment and pressed the matter no further.

However, Hudson Taylor had been boxed into a corner. This money had been given with the expectation that the CIM would send American missionaries to China. Hudson realised that it was impossible to give back money when it was not generally known who had donated it, and, if it had been given for a particular purpose, surely it should be used for that purpose. *Is God redirecting me?* he wondered. *Should I change my mind?*

He prayed about it. Then in a letter to Jennie he did seem to indicate a change of mind. 'The means for a year's support of 5 or 6 new missionaries is given or promised, and great issues are likely to result from our visit.' Next he wrote to John Stevenson saying, 'I think we must have an American branch of the Mission.'

At the beginning of August Hudson Taylor went back to

Northfield where Moody had organised a conference. There Hudson made his first direct appeal in America for men and women to go to China. Such was the desire for CIM speakers that Hudson and Howard Taylor, Reginald Radcliffe and George Studd had to each go to different towns to cope with the demand.

It was then on to Canada. On Sunday 23 September Hudson spoke at several churches in Toronto, and Radcliffe at others. These gatherings were followed by a packed and enthusiastic meeting at the YMCA hall, at which 14 Canadian CIM candidates spoke about their call to China. The next day Henry Frost and a Canadian supporter interviewed more American and Canadian applicants. Afterwards Hudson and Frost met and together formed the North American Council of CIM. By the end of September, the CIM had received over 40 applications from America and Canada, and many of these men and women had already been interviewed and accepted.

Hudson sailed from Canada on October 5 and arrived back in Shanghai at the end of the month.

In July the following year Hudson returned to America and Canada to confirm the arrangements and to cement the relationship. It was decided to establish the CIM North American headquarters in Toronto and Henry Frost moved to Canada to take up the roles of secretary and treasurer.

***

In 1874 there had been 436 Protestant missionaries of the different societies in China, well over half of whom were clustered around the treaty ports. By 1888 this had risen to 489 men, 320 married women and 231 single women, over 1,000 altogether, and they were more widely spread. Two years later CIM alone had over 400 in the field. Also by about this time it was estimated that there were over 32,000

Chinese converts. Progress was being made, but 32,000 out of 400 million people still indicated that they had barely scratched the surface of Chinese society.

CHAPTER 22

FURTHER ADVANCE

Hudson 'was in an impressionable state of mind, open to new developments ... Everything seemed possible' (John Stevenson).

The American response to CIM, and mission generally, had greatly impressed Hudson. It had further expanded his vision. To him now, as John Stevenson said, 'Everything seemed possible.'

In 1889 Hudson travelled once more to Britain, leaving Jennie in China. He also visited Sweden, Norway and America on this trip. On the journey back to China the ship stopped at Colombo. While there he wrote to Jennie, and seemed in a more solemn mood than usual. He thanked her for praying for him and then told her, 'Spiritual blessing is the one thing I want and need and must have. Given this and I have no fears. Without it nothing else will avail. May God forgive all that is wrong in me and in our Mission.'

These are startling statements from one who lived so close to God. Yet he sounds at this moment to be distant from his Lord. And if Hudson Taylor felt he needed God's forgiveness, what should the rest of us feel?

He then confessed to Jennie, 'Unwillingness to be separated from you has brought me under a cloud. I have left you unwillingly, instead of joyfully. I do want to be wholehearted in God's service.' While the thought of leaving Jennie 'joyfully' could be misunderstood, it was rather a case of being joyful at the thought of serving God faithfully, of being 'wholehearted in God's service'. They each understood that sometimes for them and the work that they were committed to these separations were necessary.

Early in 1890 the CIM opened its headquarters in Wusong Road, Shanghai. This was not one small office but three large buildings. A substantial part of the cost of this was donated by Archibald Orr Ewing, a dedicated Christian from a wealthy Scottish family. The HQ would be used to house administrative staff, and missionaries on journeys to and from other provinces and lands. It also had a 200-seat hall for conferences. Above the main entrance was a sign which said, 'To the glory of God and the furtherance of His Kingdom in China.'

John Stevenson was the senior administrator in China. This freed Hudson, who had just arrived back in China, to supervise the distribution of his missionary force and to care for them in their struggles, illnesses and dangers.

Hudson was soon faced with a new development. He had already heard from some clergy in Australia that they were interested in setting up a branch of the CIM in their country. Two days after his return Charles Parsons, a young Anglican clergyman from Australia, arrived in Shanghai. Parsons visited the CIM headquarters and asked to see Hudson Taylor. An assistant found Hudson who invited Parsons into his office and offered him a chair.

'How can I help you, Mr Parsons?'

'Mr Taylor,' he said, 'I wish to join the China Inland Mission.'

Hudson looked at him carefully. 'You are from Australia, I understand.'

'Yes, that's right. Melbourne! For some years now I have longed to take the Gospel to the Chinese. I believe that God has been calling me to do that. And Dr Macartney of my church, I believe he has written to you, is hoping to begin a branch of your Mission in Australia.'

'Yes, I've heard from Dr Macartney.'

'I have heard so much about you and your Mission, Mr Taylor. I'd love to be part of it. And I have a letter from Dr Macartney giving his support. And from ministers of other denominations too.' Parsons pulled some documents from his bag and passed them to Hudson Taylor. 'There are others in Australia thinking about coming too.'

Hudson took and examined the papers. Parsons had impressed him thus far. He was clearly dedicated to Christ and determined. 'I see.' Hudson paused. 'You are aware of our policy, I assume. Each candidate must subscribe to the essential beliefs in the Christian faith. As to baptism and such matters we allow our people to follow their consciences.'

'Yes, I know that. That's all fine.'

Hudson was still thinking. *We have spread our wings in America. And that has been blessed by God. Perhaps now is the time to do so in Australia.* 'Give me time to pray about this, Mr Parsons. I will let you know tomorrow.'

'Oh thank you, Mr Taylor. Thank you.'

'You had better stay with us tonight. I'll get someone to show you to a room.'

So, Hudson prayed about taking Charles Parsons on to the CIM staff, and about the possibility of setting up a wing of the Mission in Australia. The next day he accepted Parsons into the Mission. That May he sent a cable to Dr Macartney, saying, 'Sanction committee.' The day after the cable was received Macartney and his associates held the first meeting of the Australian Council of the CIM.

Hudson Taylor began to consider going to Australia. He realised that his presence there would add to the interest and concern about China amongst the Christian community. However, he agonised over leaving Jennie once more. *Could I, perhaps, take Jennie with me?* he wondered. *But then what would happen to our children, Ernest and*

Amy? They were only 15 and 14. They needed Jennie. But so did he.

John Stevenson was also struggling under the weight of his responsibilities. Hudson's absence would only add to them.

After an intense inward struggle, he decided to go, and he took Montague Beauchamp, one of the Seven, with him. Monty had become one of his most trustworthy helpers. They left China that July. This was to be the last time Hudson and Jennie were to be apart for any length of time until her death.

Taylor and Beauchamp attracted great crowds wherever they went; Sydney, Melbourne, where they met the newly established Council, Launceston and Hobart, Ballarat, Adelaide, Melbourne again and Brisbane. Hudson made a great personal impact upon many, though that was not his intention.

John Southey, a future CIM missionary, told his wife how disappointed he was when he first saw him. Southey had expected someone more commanding. But after his wife met Taylor she said, 'Look at the light in his face.' Southey later said that his 'first sense of disappointment gave place to deep reverence and love. We could not help noticing the utter lack of self-assertion about him.' That is a striking comment when one considers that Hudson Taylor influenced so many in the cause of Christ. He did so by love, kindness and example, rather than by bullying and domination.

When Taylor and Beauchamp left Australia late in November they were accompanied by 12 Australian candidates, four men and eight women. Meanwhile in Melbourne members of the Australian Council were interviewing another 60.

The dozen Australians were part of a much larger intake. Towards the end of 1890, in the space of less than ten weeks, 53 new CIM missionaries arrived in China from Europe, the Americas and Australia. In the first 15 weeks of the following year another 78 arrived.

Disease and danger were ongoing hazards. Anne Stevenson, the wife of John, was in poor health, which forced the Stevensons back to Scotland. Sophie Smith, the wife of Stanley, died in March 1891. At about the same time James Broumton had typhoid, and his wife had a dangerous liver abscess, though both recovered.

Hudson estimated that at this stage the CIM had posted 539 missionaries in China and most served long term. Only 44 of them were lost to the Mission after two years' service or less. Twenty-one of these died, five were too ill to continue and nine had family difficulties. Only four resigned and just four asked to withdraw. That so many laboured long, despite numerous difficulties, says much for their dedication and the strength and flexibility of the Mission that Hudson Taylor had created.

The rumour mill also kept grinding. There were reports that CIM missionaries had been forbidden to associate with other missionaries. Hudson strongly denied it. Others claimed that he was trying to turn all his missionaries into Baptists. Hudson once more denied it, and drew attention to CIM's policy that such matters as baptism were up to the individual conscience. CIM was an interdenominational mission, not a church. He pointed out that CIM had pioneered 'six organised Presbyterian churches, four Episcopal stations and four Methodist stations.' Those three denominations all practised infant baptism. There were also disputes between Hudson and the London Council.

***

Cecil Polhill had been a Lieutenant in the Dragoon Guards, and was one of the Cambridge Seven in 1885. In 1888 he married Eleanor Marsden, who had arrived in China a year before him. Hudson Taylor had plans to enter Tibet, to the west of China. With that in mind, he encouraged Cecil and Eleanor to move with their sons to the mountainous Chinese border with Tibet, which they did. However, they found entering Tibet difficult. While continuing their Chinese language studies they also began to learn Tibetan. Most of the Chinese and Tibetans in that region proved accepting and helpful, so the Polhills did not lack language teachers. However, it was a dangerous area plagued by fierce bandits.

In an attempt to take the Gospel further afield, Cecil pressed on to a new area, leaving his family at their home. The local authorities insisted that any European going into that region had to have a guide and an armed escort. He and his party came across a monastery and the leading monk welcomed them warmly.

'We have a message for you from the God of heaven,' said Cecil Polhill.

The monk smiled slightly. 'Ah, such a message we must hear,' he said, 'Wait here.'

So, Cecil waited and soon every monk in the monastery was assembled before him.

'We want to hear this message,' said the abbot. 'I have told my brothers to listen carefully and to consider it. Please tell us.'

Cecil bowed and thanked him, and began, 'I want to tell you about Jesus Christ, the Son of God.'

As he spoke, the monks listened intently. When he had finished he gave out some tracts and booklets, which were eagerly received.

Cecil returned to Eleanor and the children. A little later he went on another journey, this time with his family and two Chinese Christians named Wang and Zhang. (These appear to have been different men from the two of the same names mentioned earlier.) They reached Songpan, near the Tibetan border, and stayed there for several months. They were generally well received and even allowed to live in a small house in the town. For ten weeks all went well. The people accepted them, they listened to the preaching and accepted tracts. At first the only problem they had was yaks invading their yard.

But the region was experiencing drought, and local culture said that someone had to be to blame for that. As the drought grew worse troublemakers in the town began to stir up the people against the visitors. At first it was little more than a change of attitude, but one morning the Polhills heard an angry noise outside the house that they shared with their Chinese companions.

'Foreign devils! Foreign devils! Kill the foreign devils.'

'It sounds as though we have trouble,' Cecil said to Eleanor and the two Chinese. 'I'll go out and see if I can quieten them.'

'No, dear! No! Don't go out there. They may kill you,' cried Eleanor, her voice rising in concern.

'But I must.'

'No! No, Mr Polhill. We will go.' It was Zhang. 'They will listen to us.'

Cecil could see the sense in that, but as a soldier he was not keen on someone else fighting his battles. Outside the noise grew louder.

'We will go,' said Wang.

So, Wang and Zhang ventured outside. The mob raged!

'We have a message of peace. We mean you no harm,' shouted Wang.

But the noise grew louder, the mood fiercer.

'Kill them!'

'Stone them!'

'Throw them in the river.'

Some men at the front of the mob pounced on the two men and bound them. Others surged towards the house, battered the door down, hauled Cecil and Eleanor outside and bound them too. They tore the upper garments off all four Christians and began to beat them with sticks.

Each blow was struck with force. Blow upon blow! Each blow caused agony, increasing in intensity. Eleanor was not spared.

The two little Polhill boys hid in the house and were unmolested. But they could hear the screams of their parents and were terrified.

Then suddenly came the shout, 'Stop this! Stop this, I command you.' The shout was heard above the roar of the crowd. It was a senior officer in the army.

The mob gradually became silent.

'Let them go!' commanded the officer. 'I will take them to the mandarin. We will see what he has to say.'

So, the four were released, though with their arms still bound, and the soldier marched them off to the mandarin. The mandarin was tolerant rather than sympathetic, but he agreed to offer them protection, and they remained at his home overnight.

The next morning the people assembled again. Once more they were baying for blood. The mandarin looked out on them and for a while ignored what was going on. But the mob would not disperse and shouted, 'Bring out the foreign devils. Kill them!'

The mandarin looked and listened. He knew that he had to make a response, so he had Wang and Zhang brought before him. They bowed low.

'Someone must suffer for this crime.'

'But no crime has been committed, mandarin.'

'I said someone must suffer.' The mandarin's voice was raised to a higher pitch. He thought for a moment and then said, 'I will see that the Europeans are released and kept safe, if you will take their punishment.'

Wang and Zhang looked at each other. They knew that if they agreed to that they could suffer terribly. But they answered, 'We will. Let them go.'

The Polhills were released under armed guard to protect them. The two Chinese were taken into the public square and flogged. When the brutal punishment had been inflicted and their backs were raw they were locked into devices that fitted around their necks and restricted movement.

The next day they were all escorted out of the city.

Zhang later said, 'We were in a very small way like our master, Jesus Christ.' And so they had been.

Much later it became known that a man who had witnessed these brutal assaults, and had been deeply touched by the example of Wang and Zhang, became a believer in the Christ who had suffered for others.

***

In the early and mid-1890s the work of CIM continued to grow and to spread. CIM bases in Britain, the Americas and Australia sent more missionaries to China. Most importantly more Chinese Christians were taking the initiative of spreading the good news to their own people.

However, all this meant that Hudson Taylor was stretched to the limit. When John Stevenson arrived back in China in March 1892 he found the near sixty-year old Hudson totally exhausted. In May that year when Hudson and Jennie embarked on a trip to Canada and Britain he suffered badly from neuralgia and a gastric condition. Indeed, his stay in Canada and America was longer than originally planned to allow him to rest. Two years later he had a worse bout of neuralgia or a related condition, plus enteritis. His health was clearly beginning to fail. Jennie at about this time also had dysentery.

Not that they were the only members of CIM with health problems. In January 1892 one entire missionary family died from an undiagnosed fever. Typhoid, Typhus and Cholera were common and dangerous threats, and they did kill some CIM staff. Spasmodic persecution also broke out in various places. Being a missionary, being a Christian, in China was not easy. But it was soon to get worse.

CHAPTER 23

THE BOXER UPRISING (1899-1901)

'Precious in the sight of the Lord is the death of his saints' (Psalm 116:15).

As far as people in Britain were concerned, the Boxer Uprising in China was initially of little importance. However, it soon began to seem more disturbing.

On 27 March 1900, a Reuter's correspondent lodged a report that appeared in British newspapers more than a month later. It said that 'movements of the members of the secret society known to foreigners as Boxers appear to be assuming an alarming aspect. The latest news about their operations is that they have apparently found themselves strong enough to embark on open conflict with the Imperial troops, and that an indecisive action was fought between a body of Boxers, numbering some 1,500 men, and an equal force of troops... It is stated that losses on both sides were very heavy.'

A later brief report appeared in several British newspapers in the middle of May. It said, 'More outrages by the "Boxers" are reported sixty miles to the north of Tientsin. A number of native Christians are stated to have been massacred.' But these reports were hidden amongst the much greater coverage of the Boer War.

The Boxers were a fiercely anti-European, anti-Christian, group of Chinese fighters. They called themselves 'Fist of Patriotic Union' because they believed that with boxing and other martial and magical arts they were invincible and could drive the Westerners out of China. Hence 'Boxers' became the popular English translation of that name.

They first came into being in Shantung on the central eastern coast in May 1899 and then spread further north into Chili. As has been seen, there had long been understandable discontent about European interference in China and this dissatisfaction was growing. The opium scandal added fuel to that fire. When another famine occurred, many Chinese believed this was because the Chinese authorities tolerated the European presence.

Germany was the dominant European force in Shantung. When three Germans were attacked by Chinese villagers, the Germans responded by destroying several villages. This inevitably roused the wrath of many Chinese, both in the leadership, including the Empress Dowager Ci Xi, and in the grass-roots community. The rise of the Boxers was triggered by this event, and Ci Xi supported them. They were even able to get away with killing a mandarin who opposed them. They carried banners emblazoned with the slogan 'Kill the Foreigners!'

In the eyes of the Boxers, all Christians were foreigners. It made no difference to them that some of these Christians were as Chinese as they were. The wrath of the Boxers fell upon not just missionaries and other Europeans but also, and especially, upon Chinese Christians, because they had embraced a 'foreign' religion.

In the second half of June 1899 there were several outbreaks of Boxer violence. In Kienning in the north of Fukien a mob destroyed the CMS building, killed a Chinese Christian, and three missionaries only just managed to escape. In another town, at about the same time, the LMS and Catholic buildings were destroyed and three Catholic priests killed. Dr Frank Keller of the CIM only escaped because a Chinese official gave him protection. After his escape, Keller reported that he had heard rumours about an imperial edict to kill foreigners. *Is this just panic*, Keller wondered, *or is there a real threat?*

Late in December of that year a small band of Boxers kidnapped S. M. Brooks of the Society for the Propagation of the Gospel. When their attention was diverted, Brooks managed to escape, but the Boxers ran him down and beheaded him. Brooks was the first Protestant missionary to die in these troubles. There would be many more.

***

Hudson and Jennie Taylor were visiting Australia, New Zealand and America during this period. Hudson knew that such visits encouraged local CIM Councils, raised interest in the Mission and resulted in more people offering to take the Gospel to China.

Though he was many miles away, Hudson noted the events in China with some unease. While there had always been danger and death for Christians in China, something new appeared to be happening. However, neither the Taylors nor anyone else knew at that time how bad it would become.

In America at the end of April 1900, Hudson attended and spoke at a major Foreign Missions Conference in the Carnegie Hall in New York. Over 1,800 official delegates attended these meetings, plus hundreds of visitors. William McKinley, America's President, and Theodore Roosevelt, the Governor of New York State, were present on the first day to welcome the delegates.

Hudson Taylor gave one of the early addresses at the conference, which demonstrates how highly he was regarded by this time. His subject was the source of power for foreign mission work. His first words exploded with great force: 'Our subject this morning is the source of power for Christian mission, and, in a word, *power belongeth unto God.*' His now-frail body seemed to pulsate with life as he spoke. The massive assembly was silent, except for his lone voice.

Hudson Taylor and China

'God Himself is the great source of power,' he continued. 'It is His possession. And He manifests it according to His sovereign will; yet not in an erratic or arbitrary manner, but according to His declared purposes and promises. Further, God tells us by His prophet Daniel that the people that do know their God shall be strong and do exploits. Those who know their God do not *attempt* to do exploits, *but do them.*' He paused for a moment and stroked his bushy white beard. 'We shall search the Scriptures in vain, from Genesis to Revelation, for any command to *attempt* to do anything. God's commands are always "*Do this.*" His prohibitions are always "*Do not* do this."' Taylor's emphases were bold and forceful. Their meanings struck home to many.

'Further, God's power is an available power. We are a supernatural people, born again by a supernatural birth, kept by a supernatural power, sustained on supernatural food, taught by a supernatural Teacher from a supernatural Book.' He paused briefly to catch his breath. 'We are led by a supernatural Captain in right paths to assured victories. The risen Saviour, ere he ascended on high, said, "All power is given unto me in heaven and on earth." *Go ye therefore!* Disciple! Baptise! Teach all nations. And "Ye shall receive power when the Holy Ghost is come upon you." The power given is not a gift *from* the Holy Ghost. He, Himself is the Power.'

Hudson Taylor then went on to describe different ways in which that power was made manifest. He also gave evidences of how that power was experienced on the mission field.

Towards the end of his address he took a different tack. He said, 'Beloved, you whose duty it is to remain at home, are equally sharers with those who go into the mission fields in this work; yours the responsibility; yours equally to share in the reward when Christ is glorified.' He clearly recognised the importance of the work of people like William Berger, Benjamin Broomhall and a host of people who supported, prayed for and gave to mission.

In closing he said, 'Is not the power of prayer very much the gauge of *our* power to do God's work successfully, anywhere and under any circumstances? This power, this marvellous power, would bear much more attention than we have ever given it. We may well thank God that He has not left us difficult service without providing us abundant power, adequate power and resources for its discharge for all time, even to the end of the world. Amen!'

Hudson's message proved memorable and life changing. More than 30 years later Henry Frost said, 'I am still meeting men and women who declare that Hudson Taylor's address that morning radically changed their lives.'

In a later, briefer, address at the Conference, Hudson Taylor claimed that there were by this time about 100,000 communicant members in Chinese Protestant churches. This, as he pointed out, was a vast increase on the few hundred in the early 1850s. Not that all this was the work of the CIM, but that Mission should certainly be credited with the greater part of that. It had more men and women in the field and it had penetrated wider and further than any other mission.

A few days after that conference Hudson went to Boston for further speaking engagements. At one of these meetings he was introduced by his American friend A. T. Pierson. Hudson slowly rose to speak and began his address, but he spoke less clearly than usual. He began to stumble over his words and then started to repeat himself. Finally, he just stopped. As a doctor in the audience came to his aid, Pierson took over his address.

After that meeting one of his associates told him, 'Hudson, you must knock off work altogether for a time. You will kill yourself unless you rest.'

Hudson looked at him. 'But there is so much to do.'

'Yes! And China needs you. But you'll do more for China and Christ by resting now and then picking up the reins in a few weeks' time.'

'I know, but ...'

'Rest! You must rest.'

For the remainder of their stay in America Hudson Taylor did rest. He attended some meetings, but did not speak at them. Early in June he and Jennie embarked for Britain, but he remained unwell. It was a while before they became fully aware of the quickly deteriorating circumstances in China.

***

Back in China, in January that year, Ci Xi issued an edict supporting the Boxers. After that unruly gangs developed into an army, hundreds of thousands strong, and fists and swords became rifles and cannons. There was also plenty of other official support, and it seems that some Chinese officials offered a reward for every foreigner killed.

In the middle of May, the Boxers attacked three Catholic villages in Chili. They came screaming into each village in turn, slashing and shooting anyone not quick enough to get away. When they rounded up some of the 'escapees' they showed no mercy. They herded them into buildings and then set the buildings alight. The victims were mainly Chinese Catholics.

About a week later the Boxer 'Army' attacked two largely Protestant villages, killing the Chinese pastor and some other Christians, and destroying the chapel. At about the same time in another area a Boxer attacked Elder Si, a leading Chinese Christian, with a sword. Si was mortally wounded and died a few weeks later.

Soon after that a band of Boxers raided the home of Hsi Shengmo. He was away, but they brutally beat his wife and mother, and ransacked the building, taking away everything that was movable.

But the Boxer Uprising was just beginning. As it began to escalate some missionaries decided to move away from the dangerous areas, though others courageously stayed with their Chinese brothers and sisters.

John Stevenson was again leading CIM in China, while Hudson was away. It was probably early in June that he began to receive reports of serious trouble, with multiple deaths, from various places, but he was at first unable to verify them. Dead people do not speak, and live people often exaggerate, so for a little while he was unsure how serious the situation was. But gradually it became clear: the Boxers were a major threat to all Europeans and to Chinese Christians. The revolt, in fact, spread further and further afield, particularly in the provinces of Shantung, Chili and Shansi, and in Mongolia. The Boxers rampaged through these regions, killing foreigners and those considered sympathetic to foreigners.

In the middle of June, the Boxers turned their attention upon Peking, the Chinese capital. A large, screaming horde of Boxers broke into the city, many carrying flaming torches. They set fire to churches, chapels, cathedrals, official European offices and residences, and anything that looked foreign. They were so obsessed with their aims that they destroyed some 'innocent' Chinese buildings too.

But worse, they hunted down hundreds of Chinese Christians, Protestant and Catholic, and tortured, mutilated and killed them, burning many alive. Others who escaped the initial attack sheltered in the major buildings still standing, which by this time were barricaded and defended by small numbers of European military and any Chinese under threat who could carry a weapon.

A large force of European, American, Japanese and Sikh troops eventually marched on Peking to relieve the city, but it first had to fight to get there. The troops arrived in the middle of August in a downpour, but made their assault nonetheless.

Inside the city the Boxers were firing into the barricaded buildings. In one of these 'fortresses' near the city wall, where hundreds had sheltered for weeks with little food or medicine, the people crouched in terror. Suddenly a man cried out, 'Listen! A machine gun!'

'It's the Boxers,' said a companion, stating the seemingly obvious.

'No! No! It's coming from a different direction. And it's outside the walls.'

The second man listened. There was noise, noise and more noise: the frightening sounds of the Boxers guns firing, the sounds of bullets hitting the building that they were sheltering in, the rain, and the shouts and screams from outside and inside their sanctuary. But there, clear enough, was another sound, the persistent rat-tat, rat-tat of a distant machine gun.

Soon bullets stopped striking their building. One by one the people within began to stand up. They looked at each other. *Could the Boxers have ended their attack?* they wondered. For a few moments hardly anyone dared to speak.

One man climbed up to a broken window. 'It's chaos out there,' he shouted back to his companions. 'But the Boxers ... Well, they seem to be dashing towards the city walls. I can see men in turbans entering the city. They're Sikhs, I think. It's the relief. It's the relief! They've come to rescue us!'

For a moment there was silence within their 'fortress.' Then men, women and children, Europeans, Americans and Asians leapt to their feet and burst forth into loud cheering. Others sat down and cried tears of release.

A bloody battle to take the city followed which the allies eventually won and they rescued the thousands who had been sheltering in the reinforced buildings. Some of the allied forces then, sadly and unnecessarily, ransacked parts of the city. However, this defeat proved a major blow to the Boxers, though they remained active in other places for some months afterwards.

The Uprising had been a terrible time of death and destruction. In the period from June to October 1900, 48 CIM missionaries were killed, plus 21 of their children, and another ten adults from missions closely associated with CIM. In the same period, the Boxers killed 77 adults from other Protestant missions, plus 32 of their children. In addition, nearly 50 Catholic priests and nuns also died.

It was impossible to calculate how many Chinese Christians died and estimates vary. It is probable that several thousand Chinese Protestants died and an even higher number of Catholics. And many more Christians suffered in other ways. The wrath of the Boxers was especially fierce upon Chinese Christians. Yet many remained true to Christ despite the terror and suffering. The situation eased at the end of the year and there was much less trouble in 1901.

To deal with the perpetrators and the results of this uprising, negotiations between the Chinese and European leaders began on Christmas Eve 1900. Debate was complicated and heated, and settlement was not reached until September the following year. Various punishments were given to leaders in the uprising, which included house arrest, execution, and, in two cases, permission to commit suicide. It also became illegal for the Chinese to belong to an anti-foreign society.

While the Boxer Uprising was savage and cruel, the ways in which the European and American authorities treated the Chinese, before and after the troubles, was arrogant and unkind. It is easy to understand the discontent of the Chinese, both those of high rank and low, though one must condemn the cruelty.

***

As we have seen, Hudson Taylor was still overseas and unwell as these terrible events unfolded. Inevitably they greatly distressed him. He went to Switzerland to recuperate in July, but the bad news followed him.

One morning soon after his arrival there, Jennie was on hand when a telegram arrived from London telling news of events in China that July, including the deaths of several CIM missionaries. Jennie decided not to hand it to Hudson, but to tell him the terrible news gradually. However, he found her with this piece of paper in her hand and eagerly asked her, 'What's that, Jennie? Is it news from China?'

'Yes, Hudson, it is,' she said hesitantly. 'But it's not good, I'm afraid.'

'Let me see it. Let me see it. I must know.'

She gave him the telegram and he read the contents. As he read it he began to sway and nearly lost his balance. Jennie helped him to a seat. As he gradually recovered from the initial shock he said, 'Where will the end be?' though more to himself than Jennie.

In the weeks ahead more terrible news arrived and he wept. The loss of so many fine missionaries, Chinese Christian leaders and other Christians was a fierce blow to his sensibilities and his hopes. But he did not despair. Jenny wrote to John Stevenson on Hudson's behalf saying, 'We are all suffering with you all so much that I don't think we could feel more.'

Stevenson, meanwhile, was under great stress on the battle front. Hudson fully realised this but was unable to offer him the personal assistance that he needed, so he decided to appoint an on-the-spot General Director to act in his stead. He gave that position to Dixon Hoste, one of the Cambridge Seven. Since Hoste's arrival in China he had spent a number of years working with Hsi Shengmo, and after a period in Australia to recover from his labours he returned to China. Hudson had previously appointed him Deputy Director to John Stevenson just before the Boxer crisis.

CHAPTER 24

IT IS NOT DEATH TO DIE

'When I cannot read, when I cannot think, when I cannot even pray, then I can trust' (Hudson Taylor).

Hudson and Jennie spent the final months of 1900 in Switzerland. Hudson was still unwell but improving. When the weather became too cold they moved to Cannes in the south of France, where William Berger's widow was staying, recuperating after an illness. Her husband had died early in 1899. Also in Cannes at that time was a CIM family that had only just escaped from the Boxers. The Taylors stayed there until April and then returned to London.

Hudson did his best to keep up with affairs in China. He received a mountain of correspondence from those in the field, and dealt with as much as his health allowed. Other CIM workers had to do the remainder.

By August 1901 Hudson seemed to be recovering. He and Jennie were in Switzerland again, and Hudson was well enough to go walking. In the middle of the month he returned from a walk limping.

Jennie was immediately concerned. 'Are you alright. You don't look well.'

Hudson hesitated to answer, but then softly said, 'I think I may have had a slight stroke.'

'A stroke?'

'Yes! One side of my body feels weak. I had a fall just now.' He looked and sounded rather confused. 'I'm not quite sure what happened.'

'Come indoors,' said Jennie anxiously. 'I'll get a doctor to examine you.' Jennie helped him into the house and a doctor was called.

Whether it was a stroke or not was never determined, but it was a setback, though only a slight one. Hudson still proved able to deal with his correspondence and advise on Mission business, but his health was up and down and from this time on he was never well.

In 1902 news came of a cholera outbreak in China. Then came typhoid. These diseases killed several in the CIM team, including children.

By this time Hudson Taylor was too tired and unwell to run the Mission's affairs efficiently, so he prepared to step down as its leader. In November he put forward Dixon Hoste as his successor and this was accepted by the Council. On the first day of 1903 Hudson Taylor officially retired from the Mission he founded and loved, and Dixon Hoste became the General Director.

On the previous day Hudson had finished reading right through the Bible for the fortieth time. Scripture and the God who brought that Scripture into being meant as much to him now as they had in his youth.

Jennie was also unwell. She was becoming weaker and weaker, and had a lump on her abdomen. That July a surgeon conducted an exploratory operation on her.

Soon after the procedure Hudson was called into the surgery and was offered a seat. 'And what's the news,' he asked anxiously.

'Well, Mr Taylor, I'm afraid that your wife has an inoperable tumour in the abdomen. I'm sorry.'

Hudson was stunned. For a moment he said nothing. Jennie had been his love and great helper for 30 years, and now was he going to lose her? 'It's inoperable, you say?'

'Yes! An operation would certainly kill her.' Knowing that Hudson was a doctor, the surgeon then explained the problem in more detail.

Hudson sat there as the news settled into his mind. 'And how long?'

The surgeon hesitated. 'A year, maybe a little more.'

'And for this kind of tumour there could be pain?'

'Yes, almost certainly.'

Dr Howard Taylor, Hudson's second son, was also on hand, and he had further discussion with the surgeon. 'Father tells me that the tumour does not need to be removed.'

The surgeon paused. For a moment he looked uncertain. 'Well, that's not quite true. It's rather a case of it being dangerous. The operation would kill her.'

'Oh! I see.' Howard wondered how his father could have misunderstood. *Perhaps he was just hoping that an operation was not necessary rather than not advisable.*

From then Jennie's health gradually declined. The months passed and another year came and she became weaker and weaker. But through it all she was serene. Mercifully, there was little pain, just an ever-present tiredness.

Hudson, meanwhile, was aging fast. The many stresses of his life were now taking full toll, and the prospect of losing Jennie seemed to quicken his decline.

That July an old friend came to visit Jennie. She noticed how thin and pale she looked, yet through it all was a composed serenity. She held Jennie's hand and spoke quietly to her. 'My dear Jennie, heaven is close. Soon you will experience its joys. Are you looking forward to that, Jennie?'

Jennie's breathing was heavy and for a moment she did not speak. Then quietly but firmly she said, 'The Bible says more about Jesus than it does about heaven.' She paused to catch her breath. 'No, I do not often think about heaven.' She paused again. 'He is here with me, and He is enough.'

A few days later Hudson was sitting by her bedside, when Jennie suddenly cried out, 'No pain! No pain!'

Hudson gently held her hand and spoke tenderly to her.

She turned to him and softly said, 'Ask Him to take me quickly.' Hudson could feel the tears welling up in his eyes. He was too overcome with emotion to speak again. A few minutes later she passed into glory.

***

Hudson Taylor knew that he too was dying, but he had one final ambition. He longed to return to China and to die there. Even though he had had long absences from that land there was a real sense in which China was his home.

He first approached his son Howard with the idea. 'I must go back to China, Howard. I belong there.'

'Are you well enough, do you think, Father?'

'I've had lots of sea voyages, Howard. They haven't killed me yet.'

Howard smiled.

'And, anyway,' Hudson continued, 'I don't have long in this world, so England or China won't make much difference. The Lord will take me home soon.'

Howard could see there was no point in arguing. He knew that when his father's mind was made up, as it seemed to be, there was little chance of changing it. 'Geraldine and I are hoping to go back early next year. Why don't we all go together.'

'Yes, that makes sense. I'll advise the Council.' Then as an afterthought he said, 'Oh, and I must visit Changsha.'

Howard smiled again. He knew that Changsha was the capital of Hunan province, which had been the most persistently violent, anti-European, anti-Christian state in China. Yet news had reached them that there had been a breakthrough there and now many were listening to the Gospel and believing.

On 15 February 1905 Hudson left England for the last time.

Travelling with his son and daughter-in-law, they went via the USA, but though the journey was long it was a safer and more enjoyable voyage than many he had had.

He arrived at the CIM Headquarters at Wusong Road in mid-April. The China Council was in session at that time and John Stevenson, along with a host of CIM staff, gave him a warm welcome. Hudson could feel the tears welling up in his eyes as he looked out upon this large band of dedicated missionaries and native pastors. A lot had changed in 50 years. Then it was just a few missionaries and a handful of Chinese Christians. Now there were hundreds of missionaries scattered throughout China and many thousands of Chinese believers. Yet there was still so much more to do.

A little later he travelled to Chinkiang and visited Maria's grave. Memories flooded back. Wonderful memories! Warm, yet sad memories!

While there he addressed a group of young missionaries who had recently arrived. 'You do not know what lies before you,' he began. 'I give you one word of advice: Walk with the Lord! Count on Him! Enjoy Him! He will not disappoint you. For 40 years I have made it the chief business of my life to cultivate a personal acquaintance with the Lord Jesus Christ. That is the missionary's most important task and joy.'

Later he was having an informal meeting with some of his old colleagues, when a telegram arrived. He opened it, and read 'Joseph Edkins gone to be with Lord.' More memories! Hudson remembered his first visit to inland China in the company of Edkins. That was the first major step in his mission to China. He shared the sad news with his friends. 'Joseph Edkins?' said one. 'That man knew more about China than any of us.'

'Yes,' said Hudson, 'he did.'

At the end of May, he travelled to Hunan. Now a dozen missionary societies were active in that once strongly anti-Christian state, with over 100 missionaries. A couple of days later, as he had hoped, he arrived in Changsha, the capital. He visited the CIM premises, which was gaily decorated with banners welcoming him to the city. He felt tears welling up in his eyes as he read those messages. What a change there had been.

The next day was Saturday, June 3. A reception had been planned for that afternoon to officially welcome him to the city. At 5 p.m. he came down from his room and shared afternoon tea with about thirty people, mainly from various missionary societies. He was frail, but seemed bright and rejoiced in the conversations.

When the visitors had departed, Howard Taylor helped his father upstairs to his room, assisted him into a chair and left him there for a few minutes. Dr Barrie, another colleague, visited Hudson and they began to talk about the work.

'When I am praying, Hudson,' said Barrie, 'I sometimes think about the distinction between small things and great things. That frequently comes to my mind.'

Hudson tried to respond, but speaking was becoming difficult for him. Then softly he managed to say, 'There is nothing small; there is nothing great. Only God is great, and we should trust him fully.'

Howard returned with a tray of food. Geraldine, his wife, entered the room too. As Howard read to his father, Geraldine encouraged the old man to eat. He did not eat much, so Howard helped his father into bed and left the room. Geraldine remained and continued to talk to her father-in-law. Suddenly Hudson turned his head and gasped deeply. At first Geraldine thought he had sneezed. Then he gasped again. And again!

There was clearly a change in him. Geraldine immediately cried out, 'Howard! Come quickly. Come quickly.'

The urgency in her voice brought her husband running in, followed by another doctor. They rushed to the side of dear Hudson Taylor, but there was nothing they could do. He took another deep breath and died.

A great man of God had gone to be with his Lord.

EPILOGUE

Hudson Taylor 'was able to care for a baby, cook a dinner, keep accounts, and comfort the sick and sorrowing, no less than to originate great enterprises and afford spiritual leadership to thoughtful men and women' (Howard and Geraldine Taylor).

James Hudson Taylor is rightly regarded as one of the great men of the Christian missionary movement. He has been the human inspiration for thousands to offer themselves for missionary service, both in his lifetime and since. He was a great man. Many, many tributes have been paid to him over the years since he died. But the greatest tribute to him today is the Church in China, for he did more than any other individual to take the Gospel to that nation.

Since the time of Hudson Taylor's ministry, Protestant Christianity in China has experienced times of difficulty and persecution but has also had some remarkable triumphs. In the years immediately after his death the Protestant Church continued to grow, but there was still much opposition.

Less than ten years after Taylor's death the First World War began, which, apart from its many tragedies, robbed China and other parts of the world of a host of missionaries. Many Christians who were considering the call of God on their lives felt that they had to go and fight for King and country, and many of them died. However, the CIM membership still increased to about 1,300 by 1932.

The Treaty of Versailles after the First World War also did not smile favourably on China, even though China had fought on the side of the allies. This alienated many Chinese. In 1921 the Chinese Communist Party was founded, which proved more significant than was realised at the time. The 1930s saw the rise of the Communist Party in China and its war with the nationalist forces of Chiang Kaishek. Many missionaries and Chinese Christians were caught up in this and some died.

The worst period, however, was after Mao Zedong took charge of China in 1949. At that time there were about one million Protestant Christians in the country and three million Catholics. In 1950, as part of its campaign against foreign influence and to control Christianity in China, the Communist government introduced the Three-Self Patriotic Movement. This was a state controlled church, with its three pillars being self-governance, self-support and self-propagation. As this church operated under state control it was seriously compromised. In addition, the theology of the Three Self Church was distinctly liberal. However, many Christians endeavoured to remain independent of that movement and some were imprisoned for their stand.

Persecution became more severe during the cultural revolution of 1966. Churches were closed, many believers were martyred or imprisoned, and the remainder went underground. But in 1979 Deng Xiaoping came to power and introduced a more tolerant approach and churches were reopened.

In 1980 when some Christians from Hong Kong visited Wenchow in the province of Chekiang they found 50,000 Christians. Chekiang was the first province that Hudson Taylor focused on, and Wenchow a town in which CIM had made a significant early impact.

The Three Self Church continues to function and today many of its members have an evangelical theology. However, it is probable that about two-thirds of today's Protestant Christians in China meet in churches outside the Three-Self Movement. These are often called 'house churches', but some have congregations of hundreds or even thousands, which rather stretches the meaning of that term.

Today it is believed that there are somewhere between 70 and 100 million Protestant Christians in China, and, remarkably, it is possible that there will soon be more Christians in China than in the USA. This is the great triumph of Chinese Christianity. Despite persecution the church in China has grown into a strong, though diverse, body. There is also now a massive printery in Nanking, which prints millions of Bibles and other Christian material in Chinese. This was an initiative of Chinese Christians, but now has the support of the United Bible Societies and Christians from around the world.

There have been ongoing sporadic outbursts of persecution in the country but this has often been localised rather than nationwide. However, in 2015 the Chinese authorities began a more energetic anti-Christian campaign, a notable feature of which was pulling down the crosses on churches. This campaign increased during 2016.

Hudson Taylor was not the first Protestant missionary to enter China. But it is fair to say that he played the most significant part in taking the Gospel of Jesus Christ into inland China and shaping the destiny of Christianity in that land. Since his death other missionaries and many thousands of Chinese have expanded that work, often in the most difficult and stressful of circumstances. But Hudson Taylor's name still stands greatly honoured in the history of Christianity in China.

In 1964 the China Inland Mission extended its activities to other countries, mainly in eastern Asia, and changed its name to the Overseas Missionary Fellowship (OMF). Today it serves in many countries in East Asia, plus in many other lands where Asians are found. John Pollock said, 'The spirit and personality of [Hudson] Taylor permeate the CIM/OMF still,' in *Hudson Taylor & Maria* (Fearn, Tain: Christian Focus, 2015), p.10. And so it does.